NOW YOU KNOW
NASHVILLE

2nd Edition

The Ultimate Guide To The Pop
Culture Sites And Sounds That Made
Music City!

MASON DOUGLAS

Wild Cataclysm Press
PO Box 128441
Nashville, TN 37212
www.NowYouKnowNashville.com

Ordering Information: Quantity sales. Special discounts are available on quantity purchases by corporations, associations, hotels, tourist bureaus, conventions, and others. For details, contact the publisher at the address above. Orders by U.S. trade bookstores and wholesalers. Please contact NowYouKnowNashville@gmail.com or visit www.NowYouKnowNashville.com.

Printed in the United States of America

Second Edition

Please visit www.NowYouKnowNashville.com

TABLE OF CONTENTS

<u>To my Mom...</u>
who gave me the passion to read.

*With a very special "Thank You" to Judy
Harris and Karen Sturgeon, who gave me the
chance to write.*

INTRODUCTION

So you think you know Nashville, huh?

Or maybe you *want* to know Nashville. Either way, you've come to a very unique place in your search for some pretty darn cool things about Nashville! 'Cuz this book is all about the "places" – the exact spots and locations where history took place and songs were written as Music City evolved. What you are holding is the 2nd Edition of a labor of love in my world – the result of now many years of researching, traveling, photographing, and discovering one of the greatest and culturally rich cities in the world, Nashville, Tennessee. As a touring musician, my absolute favorite part of traveling is finding out "What happened here?" in any given city...what are the sites, the movie locations, the infamy, the food, the history. I've tracked down hundreds of sites from the Top Gun barbeque in San Diego to Stephen King's "IT" standpipe in Bangor, ME...the cabin from "Evil Dead" in Tennessee to the actual rock in Blue John

Canyon in Utah where Aron Ralston was trapped before cutting off his own arm. So, to pay tribute to all the cool spots in Nashville, I started digging up all the dirt I could and asking songwriters about the stories behind their songs, as well as where they wrote them. That led to being driven up and down Music Row by the great Jerry Kennedy, "checking crops" with Jerry Bradley, exploring "ground zero" at the Quonset Hut, standing in Garth's vocal booth at Jack's Tracks, hanging with the ghosts in Marty Robbins' attic office, bushwhacking like Timothy Demonbreun through Shelby Bottoms Park, and simply getting introduced to some of the greatest songwriters and producers that have ever worked in this town. It was a truly humbling and surreal experience that I am grateful for.

Now here are the old-fashioned disclaimers: What you will find in this book is strictly for entertainment value. These are the "best of their knowledge" recollections from some of the folks who were there. Sometimes the story is a little fuzzy (as one interviewee stated, "I'm not sure – I was drunk a lot back then..."), sometimes it's crystal clear. The research has been confirmed and verified to the _best of all of our abilities_ but there might be a fact or two along the way that is simply the way _that_ person remembers it but not necessarily the way somebody else remembers it. And there's nothing wrong with that. As they say in songwriting, "Never let the truth get in the way of a good story." But I can assure you that the locations themselves are indeed factual, since they are the overall point of this book.

I should also continue to point out that, much like William Goldman's _The Princess Bride_, this is the "good parts version" of Nashville history. Even with over 400 locations, we're still only skimming the surface of the incredible history of this town...and each entry is only a _very_ brief summary of the actual history that is behind each event. There are far more in-depth looks at many of the subjects in this book so please pick up _those_ books as well for a much more detailed experience of anything that piques your interest.

I also know that a good many Nashvillans, upon browsing this volume, will wonder incredulously why *their* knowledge and information was not collected. To them I say, bring it on! We're just getting started here and I'd absolutely love to know what you know – that is why there are 2nd, 3rd, 4th editions in the book world. Simply email your info at NowYouKnowNashville@gmail.com and we'll talk. The wonderful thing about history is that it's always being made. There are so many more sites to find and so much more Nashville pop culture to document. Thank you for reading this book and I hope you enjoy the ride!

So you think you know Nashville? Well, let's find out...

~Mason Douglas   *March 25, 2012 – Dec 30, 2015*

HISTORY

"Here is the extensive country; we shall find no better."
~James Robertson, 1780, as recorded by John Haywood

Nashville is steeped in a unique history that has shaped not only itself but many other parts of the state, the country, and the world. If Timothy Demonbreun had not seen a herd of buffalo on the site of modern-day downtown...if the Union hadn't solidified it's momentum of the Civil War in the Battle of Nashville...if Owen and Harold Bradley had not started churning out hits in their little aluminum Quonset hut in a non-descript residential neighborhood...well, needless to say, Nashville and it's place in the world of Country music would look a whole lot different today. Here are a few sites that can be credited to giving Nashville its notable history.

ACME FEED AND SEED

101 Broadway
www.AcmeNashville.com

One of two lower Broadway building on the National Historic Registry (the other being the legendary Ryman Auditorium), this multistory historical landmark building stood vacant for over 20 years until Alan Jackson and some other investors decided to renovate the space in 2014 and create Acme Feed and Seed. Aside from the notable history as a community gathering space and an industrial icon, the interior is what makes this place so special – the support beams are from trees from Andrew Jackson's property...the Acuff-Rose sign hangs in the 2nd story wall...historic brass plates explain the history of bar counters...and the guys from American Pickers helped with the décor. The food is fantastic and there's music constantly happening so it's a go-to spot for any traveler and/or local to get a unique taste of Nashville. Tom Cruise was even spotted on the rooftop here in 2015 during the town's historic 4th of July fireworks celebration.

ACUFF-ROSE

220 Capitol Blvd
2510 Franklin Road

220 Capitol Blvd housed the earliest incarnation of the publishing powerhouse, Acuff-Rose. These are the rooms where the Nashville publishing industry essentially started and grew to unimaginable success as Roy Acuff and Hank Williams' hits kept coming.

Acuff-Rose eventually outgrew this room and moved to a much bigger office complex at 2510 Franklin Road, which housed multiple publishing companies, a state-of-the-art recording studio, and Hickory Records. Over the years, Acuff-Rose has held the catalogs of Williams, Lefty Frizzell, Roy Orbison, Felice and Boudleaux Bryant, The Everly Brothers, Mickey Newbury, and literally countless others. Acuff-Rose has long since been absorbed into the Music Row-based Sony/ATV Publishing but it's catalog of songs still dominates the publishing world and this landmark still stands.

BICENTENNIAL CAPITOL MALL STATE PARK
600 James Robertson Pkwy

This 19-acre state park was created to commemorate Tennessee's 200-years of statehood, with its impressive design highlighting the State Capitol building on the south side. Littered with time capsules, walking paths, and historical surprises around every corner, it's worth a visit and a look at some of the highlights of the park.

COURT OF 3 STARS AND BELL CARILLON
– North end of the park
Like the color scheme of the Tennessee flag, this portion of the park is made of red, white, and blue granite representing the 3 grand divisions of the state: East, Middle, and West Tennessee. More uniquely, a 95-bell Carillon (pillars with

bells at the tops of the towers) rings every hour, answered by a 96th bell on the State Capitol, representing the 95 counties of Tennessee and its musical heritage.

GRANITE MAP OF TENNESSEE
– South entrance of park
This 200-foot map of Tennessee is the largest in the state, if not the world. Features include counties, rivers, and roads.

McNAIRY SPRING
– West side of park at year 1796 on the Pathway Of History
This water monument is in the approximate spot of the original McNairy Spring (along with Sulphur Spring), both of which still flow under the bike trail that extends eastward toward the Cumberland River.

PATHWAY OF HISTORY
– West side of park
This 1,400 foot wall has notable events of history, from prehistoric to modern times, that have shaped the region. A break in the wall at the time of the Civil War represents the divisive nature of the state at the time.

WORLD WAR 2 MEMORIAL
– Northwest area of park
A moving tribute to the military and the lost soldiers of the war. A highlight of Bicentennial's World War 2 Memorial is an 18,000 pound granite globe that floats on 1/8 inch of water.

ZERO MILE MARKER
– Granite Map Plaza (south end)
The Nashville Automobile Club established this spot as the "zero point" for all state roads and guide books.

CENTENNIAL PARK
2500 West End Ave

This land previously known as Cockrill Springs was once the farmland belonging to Ann Robertson Johnson Cockrill, the wife of John Cockrill and the sister of General James Robertson. It was here that she organized the first schooling for pioneer children, thus becoming Tennessee's first schoolteacher and even Nashville's first Sunday school teacher. Ann had been granted the land after heroic efforts in an Indian attack on Fort Watauga; throughout the years, the grounds have been the state fairgrounds, a racetrack, a public park, and perhaps most notably, the site of the 1897 Tennessee Centennial and International Exposition, which brought about a number of exhibits like a pyramid and the well-known replica of the Parthenon.

CHEEKWOOD
1200 Forrest Park Dr.
www.Cheekwood.org

Built in 1932 and designed by New York architect Bryant Fleming, this mansion was the private home of Leslie Cheek, and his wife, Mabel. Leslie and Mabel had wisely invested in a company Leslie's cousin, Joel Cheek, had started. Joel was blending and marketing his own coffee, which was named after the most famous hotel in Nashville...the Maxwell House.

When General Foods (then Postum) bought the coffee company from the Cheeks for $40 million, Leslie and Mabel commissioned Fleming to design and build the house and grounds that you see today. In 1960, the property and

5

mansion were opened as an art museum and botanical gardens, funded and managed by a number of civic groups such as the Horticulture Society of Middle Tennessee and the Exchange Club of Nashville. Cheekwood famously features the largest collection of Worcester porcelain in America.

Paid tours are offered Tuesday through Sunday.

CIVIL WAR

BATTLE OF NASHVILLE

The Battle of Nashville was one of the most decisive of what some Nashvillians call the "War of Northern Aggression": the Civil War. It was the last stand of the Confederacy and their final chance to retake the strategically imperative city from Union occupiers. Confederate General John Bell Hood had moved his army north from Atlanta, where he had recently suffered a devastating loss to Sherman, and hoped to control Nashville, restock his supplies and move northward to further split the Union. Things did not go quite as planned for General Hood and he was driven back by Union General George Thomas and defeated over the two days of December 15 and 16, 1864.

You can follow the fascinating Civil War Trail throughout nearby middle Tennessee and see incredible history in the Battlefields: the Stones River National Battlefield, the Spring Hill Battlefield, the Franklin Battlefield. All are a short drive from downtown Nashville and offer a rich insight into Middle Tennessee's importance in the Civil War.

Very near downtown, though, are several key points of the Battle Of Nashville that are worth taking a look at.

CIVIL WAR
Battle of Nashville—Confederate Line
1808 Woodmont Boulevard

Inscribed: Trenches about 20 feet north of this point held by Loring's Division, were the center of the Confederate main line before the Battle of Nashville. On December 15, 1864, Redoubt No. 1, a  key artillery salient 200 yards NW, fired on Federal forces until overrun by General Wood's troops late in the day, when Confederates retreated toward Granny White Pike. ~ 1992 by The Historical Commission of Metropolitan Nashville and Davidson County. Marker No. 89.

CIVIL WAR
Battle of Nashville—Shy's Hill
4619 Benton Smith Road

Inscribed: On this hill was fought the decisive encounter of the Battle of Nashville December 16, 1864. At 4:15 p.m. a Federal assault at the angle on top of the hill broke the Confederate line. Col. W M. Shy, 20th  Term. Inf., was killed and Gen. T B. Smith was captured. The Confederates retreated over the Overton Hills to the Franklin Pike. ~1967 by The Historical Commission of Metropolitan Nashville and Davidson County. Marker No. 5

CIVIL WAR
Battle of Nashville—Peach Orchard Hill
approx 792 Harding Place, at intersection of Peach Orchard Dr.

Inscribed: On Dec. 16, 1864, Gen. S.D. Lee's Corps, Army Of Tennessee, held this right flank of Hood's defense line which ran south along the crest of this ridge. Violent artillery fire and infantry attacks by the corps of Wood and Steedman failed to dislodge the defenders who withdrew only after the collapse of the Confederate left and center in late afternoon. ~1970 The Historical Commission of Metropolitan Nashville and Davidson County No. 37

CIVIL WAR
Battle of Nashville—Confederate Final Stand
approx 823 Tyne Blvd.

Inscribed: After the withdrawal from the main Confederate line at Peach Orchard Hill, Lt. Gen. Stephen D. Lee formed a battle line across Franklin Pike 400 yards east of here with 200 men from the remnants of Brig. Gen. Henry Clayton's division and two cannons from the Eufaula Light Artillery. This last line of defense halted the Federal pursuit for the night as the Confederate army retreated through

the hills to the southwest.
~2008 by The Historical Commission of Metropolitan
Nashville and Davidson County. Marker No. 134

CIVIL WAR
BATTLE OF NASHVILLE – STEWART'S LINE
E side of Lealand Ln S of Battery Ln @ old Kirkman Lane.

Inscribed: Loring's division of Stewart's Corps, Hood's
confederate Army of Tennessee, fought behind this stone
wall Dec. 16, 1864. All Federal attacks were beaten back
until the Confederate line was broken a mile to the west.
The division retreated south through the hills toward
Brentwood. Erected: 1968

CIVIL WAR
BATTLE OF NASHVILLE – REDOUBT 1
Benham Ave, just north of Woodmont on west side.

This Confederate redoubt was one of 5 redoubts built by
Hood's Confederate Army in its attempted siege of Nashville
and was the last one to fall in the battle. It has been
carefully preserved by the Battle of Nashville Preservation
Society and is definitely worth a few minutes to walk
through to experience the history. The trenches can still be
seen and there are interpretive signs explaining the scenario
that surrounded the area during the battle.

CIVIL WAR
BATTLE OF NASHVILLE MONUMENT
Granny White Pike and Battlefield Dr.

Located in the heart of the land where the Battle of Nashville took place, this statue was designed by Giuseppe Moretti, erected in 1926, and pays tribute to both Union and Confederate soldiers.

CIVIL WAR
MCGAVOCK CONFEDERATE CEMETERY

1345 Carnton Ln.
Franklin, TN

McGavock Confederate Cemetery is the largest private cemetery dedicated to 1,481 Confederate soldiers that died in the Battle Of Franklin.

CIVIL WAR
MOUNT OLIVET CEMETERY

1101 Lebanon Pike

One of the oldest cemeteries in middle Tennessee, Mount Olivet Cemetery is a visual spectacle as well as the final resting place for many who have made their mark on Nashville history. The centralized Confederate Circle holds the remains of nearly 1500 Confederate soldiers from the Civil War, while the rest of the memorial garden is the burial site for names like:

Thomas Ryman
Vern Gosdin
Fred Rose
David Lipscomb
Benjamin Franklin
Cheatham
(Civil War Confederate
Major General)
Cornelia Clark Fort (aviation pioneer)
Randall McGavock (Confederate Army Officer)
John Overton
Hattie "Tootsie" Ross (of "Tootsie's Orchid Lounge" fame)

The cemetery is open daily and admission is free.

CIVIL WAR
NATIONAL CEMETERY
1420 Gallatin Pike South, Madison TN

This site was chosen by General George H. Thomas, a Union General who stated "no one could come to Nashville from the north and not be reminded of the sacrifices that had been made for the preservation of the Union" in regards to its location on the main railroad line between Louisville and Nashville.

Today, over 33,000 veterans, their spouses, and dependents are laid to rest here, 4,000 of whose identities are unknown.

The cemetery is open daily from dawn until dusk and has an Administration office with information available from 8:00 to 4:30, Monday through Friday.

CIVIL WAR
SPRING HILL BATTLEFIELD
Kedron Road, Spring Hill, TN

One of the most controversial "battles" in the Civil War took place at what is today known as the Spring Hill Battlefield...although there was hardly any battling at all and primarily served as the precursor to the Battle of Franklin.

Lt. Gen. John Bell Hood's Confederate "Army of Tennessee" was chasing Major Gen. John M. Schofield's Union armies retreat from Columbia in hopes of denying their return back to Nashville. Despite Hood's advantageous position ahead of Schofield, the Union army was able to slip past Hood in the night while he and his men...slept.

CIVIL WAR
STONES RIVER NATIONAL BATTLEFIELD
3501 Old Nashville Hwy. Murfreesboro, TN
www.nps.gov/stri

The Battle of Stones River claims the highest percentage of casualties of any Civil War battle. Developed at the urging of President Lincoln who badly needed a victory to bolster support for his Emancipation Proclamation, it was a ferocious fight of which the Union ultimately claimed victory due to the Confederates retreat. Any clear victor was technically inconclusive as the battle claimed 24,645 casualties (killed and wounded) over a 3-day campaign, the highest percentage of any Civil War battle.

Today, the battlefield is a National Park, centered around the land at the heart of the battle but still a fragment of the actual site. Numerous monuments mark the sites of the battle, such as Hazen Brigade Monument, the oldest intact Civil War memorial, which commemorates the Union men that did not retreat during attacks on Hell's Half Acre. The National Cemetery is the final resting place of 6,100 Union soldiers, 2,500 of them unknown. A driving tour takes visitors near a few of these sites while an interactive walking trail guides them further into the field of battle. Nearby Murfreesboro offers further history as well.

CLUB DEL MOROCCO
2417 Jefferson St and I-40

If one were to take eastbound I-40 exit onto Jefferson Street, one would drive through the phantom front doors of the once great Club Del Morocco. Jefferson Street hosted a number of smoky clubs and intimate venues where it was not unusual to see Little Richard, Nat King Cole, Duke Ellington, and Ella Fitzgerald perform. The famous Blue Room at the Club Del Morocco had perhaps the most energy, as word spread quickly about their house band, the King Kasuals, and their guitarist "Marbles". His mama knew him as "Jimmy" but the world knew him better as Jimi Hendrix.

The insertion of the interstate system rerouted businesses around Jefferson Street, spelling the end of the Del Morocco along with over 125 businesses.

14

DUTCHMAN'S CURVE TRAIN WRECK

Richland Creek Greenway – off of White Bridge Pike, 1/3 of a mile west of Harding Pike

The deadliest rail accident in U.S. history occurred at Dutchman's Curve, west of downtown Nashville on July 9, 1918, killing 101 people and injuring 171 others.

At 7:15 that morning, the No. 4 train, traveling from Nashville to Memphis, failed to wait for the No. 1 train, en route from Memphis to Nashville, and the two NC&StL railway trains collided at nearly 60 miles per hour. Miscommunication and procedure errors resulted in the two trains sharing a 10-mile long single stretch of track, culminating in a crash that could be heard over 2 miles away. Tragically ironic, this was to be the engineer of the No. 4 trains final run before retirement.

The wreck site is still accessible via the Richland Creek Greenway, just off of White Bridge Road. A wayside offers a brief history of the event and also showcases a few artifacts along with the existing abutments from the original stretch of track.

EAST NASHVILLE FIRE

Oldham St behind the old Seagraves Planning Mill (214 N. 1st St) now East Park

Arguably the most disastrous, if not the most famous, fire in Nashville history happened on March 22, 1916 at this spot. The cause of the fire is unknown – some suspect the tenant of the building, Seagraves and Company Planning Mill, while others suspect children running amuck - but what is known is that it destroyed 648 structures over 32 blocks across nearly 2.5 miles of East Nashville. Against all odds, only one life was lost. No traces can be found today except for East Park, built over the ruins on Woodland St.

FIRST AIRFIELD

2305 Hampton Ave

Inscription: E. L. Hampton's pasture became "Hampton Field" when transient airplanes began landing here during the first World War. About 2,000 feet long from here west, bounded north and south by Golf Club Lane and Woodmont Boulevard, it continued in use as Nashville's first airfield about five years until the opening of Blackwood Field in 1921. Erected 1970 by The Historical Commission of Metropolitan Nashville and Davidson County. Marker Number 31.

FIRST MASONIC TEMPLE

NW corner of Church Street and 4th Ave N., SW corner of the building

Inscription: Across the alley stood the first Masonic Hall in the state, designed by architect Hugh Roland in 1818.

Marquis de la Fayette was entertained there in 1825 by Past Grand Master Andrew Jackson. The 17th General Assembly of Tennessee met there in 1827. The

structure, much used as a civic center, burned in 1856. The rebuilt hall was used as a hospital supply store by Federal troops during the Civil War. Tennessee Historical Commission. Marker Number 3A 186

FISK JUBILEE SINGERS

Jubilee Hall, 17th Ave N & Jefferson St

Fisk University opened in 1866 as the first university in American to offer a liberal arts education "irrespective of color" of the students. Within 5 years, the school was broke and looking for a way to raise funds. George L. White, the school treasurer and music professor created a 9-member choral ensemble of students and went on tour to earn these funds. They left for their first tour on October 6, 1871, now celebrated annually in Tennessee as "Jubilee Day".

Battling hostility, skepticism, and racism, the group spent the next year touring small towns and slowly winning over the predominantly white audiences with their performances. During a particular exhausting stretch of the tour, Mr. White nicknamed the group the "Jubilee Singers", after a Biblical reference in an effort to raise their spirits. The group persevered and gradually earned enough money to send back to the university.

By the end of 1872, the Jubilee Singers had sung at the World Peace Festival and even the White House for President Grant. Funds raised in 1873 helped to construct Jubilee Hall, the school's first permanent building, which is now a National Historic Landmark. Today, it houses a floor-to-ceiling portrait of the original Jubilee Singers, which was a gift from England's Queen Victoria to Fisk after their 1873 tour.

FORT NASHBOROUGH

On 1st Avenue North 0.1 miles south of Church Street, on the right when traveling north.

The fort that used to stand here has been demolished since the initial printing of this book. The original fort used to stand on the banks of the Cumberland, stretching  up Church street toward 2nd Ave. The original historical sign reads:

Inscription: The original stockade fronted on the river slightly north of here, covering an area of about two acres. In that

18

enclosure, on May 13, 1780, representatives of this and other settlements met and adopted the Cumberland Compact for the government of the new settlement. About 500 yards west, April 2, 1781, settlers, assisted by dogs, drove off the Indians in the Battle of the Bluffs. Tennessee Historical Commission. Marker Number 3A 33

FORT NEGLEY
1100 Fort Negley Blvd

Fort Negley, named for General James S. Negley, was a Union outpost built in 1862 that made Nashville the most fortified city in North America at the time. It's innovative design of bombproof bastions, redans, and triangular parapets made the fort virtually impenetrable. While its cannons fired the first shots of the Battle of Nashville in 1864, another point of interest is that it deteriorated into severe disrepair since the people of Nashville had no desire to commemorate a Union Fort. It was eventually reconstructed and reopened in 2004.

FOUNDING OF NASHVILLE

Intersection of 1st Avenue North and Church Street, on the right when traveling north on 1st Avenue North.

While this author would enjoy nothing more than to describe the moment of inception of the great city of Nashville in his own words, none speak it better than the plaque that marks the spot of this great meeting.

Inscription: On Monday, April 24, 1780, two pioneers, James Robertson and John Donelson, shook hands upon the completion of a reunion at the site on which you now stand. Each man, one by land, the other by water, played out in a two-fold plan for a new settlement that grew into present-day Nashville. Robertson, at the head of his mounted band of 226 frontiersmen, traversed the long, circuitous overland route through Kentucky and Tennessee down to the Great Salt Lick. His group arrived on Christmas Day, 1779, about the time that Donelson's flotilla left Fort Patrick Henry, and at once set about preparing a place for the boatmen, women, and children who were to join them later.

Robertson, as one of the earliest and most resourceful frontiersmen of early Tennessee history, had long realized that the rolling country and rich bottomland of middle Tennessee would be an ideal location for a settlement. Although much warfare and violence were inevitable, it was his ability to deal with the Indians and their mutual respect and admiration for him that made this venture possible. He said, "we are the advance guard; our way is westward across the continent." But civilization could only begin with the river-borne families that were to come in the spring. In four months these families floated the entire extent of the Tennessee River, then turned north to the Ohio and came up the Cumberland to the Great Salt Lick - a 1000-mile trip unequalled in the annals of American history. This flotilla was headed by the courageous Colonel John Donelson on his flagship Adventure. He triumphed over freezing weather, the treacheries of a river at the highest in its history, pestilence, and savage Indians to reach his April rendezvous. This achievement has immortalized his name, for he managed it so well that no man could have done it better. His responsibilities were great because he had in his charge a large percentage of non-combatants.

In this memorial group each man stands as a representative of the hardy souls he led to fulfill a magnificent destiny. In this historic handshake each brave pioneer finds his place in history. No city should be indifferent to its founding, no people to its history, especially when so full of heroic action and noble deeds as is the history of Nashville. If space were available the name of every signer of the Cumberland Compact should be here; these two men stand witness to their toil and devotion.

This statue, commissioned by Mayor Ben West in 1962, was erected here in the fort where they met the flowering spring day of long ago. This statue is intended to keep their memory green and our love for them tender and profound. These men are the trees; we are their fruit. Erected 1962 by Mayor Ben West and the Metro Historical Commission.

21

GEOGRAPHIC CENTER OF TENNESSEE

Just north of intersection of Old Lascasses Rd and Hazelwood St, on the east side of Old Lascassas Rd. in Murfreesboro, TN.

Inscription: In 1834, the State of TN hired Professor James Hamilton to find its geographic center in order to locate the state capital as near as possible to the center of the state. However, certain circumstances and politics left the capital in Nashville, although Gov. James K. Polk wanted it moved to Murfreesboro. In 1976, 1/2  mile N.E. on Old Lascassas Rd. an obelisk was placed by the Rutherford County Historical Society at the state's geographic center. Tennessee Historical Commission. Marker Number 3A 166.

GRANNY WHITE GRAVE

Intersection of Granny White Pike and Traveler's Ridge Dr.

Lucinda White, known to most as "Granny White", set up shop just a few steps to the north of this spot in 1803 where she attracted travelers from the nearby Natchez Trace with warm beds and warm bourbon. She made enough of a mark to have one of the most memorable streets in Nashville named after her: Granny White Pike, which runs straight through her former property and becomes 12th Ave

22

S a few miles up the road. Granny White's grave now marks the spot.

GREAT FRENCH LICK
504 Jefferson St.

This spot is the earliest record of true pop culture in Nashville and marks the location of the first known white settlers in the area. Timothy Demonbreun first stumbled upon the area around 1769 when, as he was exploring via the Cumberland River, he noticed a creek (the Lick Branch) that was dispelling muddy water...a sign to any worthy hunter that bison were drinking from a water source nearby.

Demonbreun anchored, went ashore and set foot on the future site of Nashville. Not only did he find a multitude of game, but he also found the Big Salt Lick, aka the Great French Lick: a natural spring of cool sulphur water that attracted the animals to the area. Demonbreun also discovered a cabin nearby that was inhabited by a French fur trader, Charles Charleville, who had inherited the cabin from a previous tenant, a fur trader (name unknown) who had been there since 1710.

This area is the richest in true Nashville history...from Demonbreun's first steps on the banks of the Cumberland to the settlement around the springs, here lie the deepest roots of the city. Today, the Germantown Vista Apartment complex sits on the site of the original trading post – the original springs occupied the land a few hundred yards away, south of Jackson St, between 4th and 5th Ave N. The Music City Bikeway follows the approximate path of the springs from the McNairy Spring in Bicentennial Park, through the Sulphur Springs Bottom area, and into the Cumberland River. There is also a fountain on the site of the old spring, which was unfortunately covered over in the 1800's to help control irrigation.

However, the Lick Branch creek still flows under foot and the outlet into the Cumberland that first attracted Timothy Demonbreun's eye can still be seen.

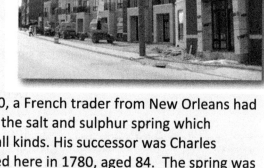

Inscription: "In 1710, a French trader from New Orleans had a trading post near the salt and sulphur spring which attracted game of all kinds. His successor was Charles Charleville, who died here in 1780, aged 84. The spring was about 300 yards southwest; the trading post was on this spot."

THE HERMITAGE

4580 Rachels Lane
www.TheHermitage.com

The home of President Andrew Jackson still holds as much reverence and fascination today as it did when Jackson, his wife, Rachel, their family and 150 slaves lived on the sprawling 1,120 acre cotton plantation. The historical value of the Hermitage is unparalleled, especially considering that

it has been painstakingly refurbished to its grand condition with as much of the original furniture, wallpaper, and artwork on display as possible.

On the grounds, the cabins known as the "First Hermitage", where Andrew and Rachel lived before the mansion was built are still standing...the springhouse still covers the original spring...the garden built by Andrew specifically for Rachel still blooms. And the bed where Andrew Jackson died in 1845 still occupies his bedroom. His tomb lies in a quiet corner of Rachel's Garden, under a monument cupula.

THE HERMITAGE
ANDREW JACKSON TOMB

Andrew Jackson's tomb lies in the southeast corner of the estate garden of the Hermitage, next to his beloved wife, Rachel. Jackson had the garden built for Rachel and named it after her: the very original "Rachel's Garden". When she died relatively suddenly in 1828, just as Andrew had been elected president, he was devastated and blamed the stresses of his political life for her death. He had Rachel laid to rest in her garden, built the gazebo monument over her grave, and is said to have visited her every day. Andrew Jackson himself died in 1845 and was placed right by her side.

The tomb has been visited by 15 million visitors, including President Reagan, and both Teddy and Franklin D. Roosevelt. Nearby are the graves of numerous other family members and even Alfred, Jackson's longtime slave and caretaker of the Hermitage.

JAMES POLK HOME
West side of 7th Ave N between Union and Church

The former home of President James K Polk stood on this site up until 1901. Polk died at this house in 1849 and his wife, Sarah, lived there until her death in 1891. Polk was buried on the site but his body was moved to the Capital property when construction of a YWCA began in 1904.

JAMES POLK TOMB
Northeast lawn of the Tennessee State Capitol, 600 Charlotte Ave.

The bodies of President James K. Polk and Sarah Polk were moved here from their property on 7th Ave N. when their former home was demolished.

26

JOLLY ROGER
209 Printers Alley

Jimi Hendrix once said, "That's where I learned to play really...Nashville, TN". The walls of this room were front and

center to witness this history, as Hendrix would often play here when it was known as the "Jolly Roger". His band, the King Kasuals, had a steady gig at the Club Del Morocco down on Jefferson St. but they were trying to stretch their horizons and look for new angles. On occasion, they booked themselves at the Jolly Roger, renamed themselves the Sandpipers, and had a certain opening act called "Jimi Hendrix and his Magic Guitar", one of the first instances of his "Jimi" moniker.

At the time of this writing, the club is now the Nashville Dinner Theater but the original stage, ceiling beams, back wall, and front door to the club reside on display at the Musician's Hall Of Fame in downtown Nashville.

MARATHON AUTOMOTIVE
1305 Clinton St.

The building itself was built in 1881 as a cotton mill but history will remember it as the manufacturing plant for the quick-lived Marathon automobile. At the time, in 1904, Marathon was the largest automobile

manufacturer in the U.S. However, production halted in

1914 and only 8 Marathon cars are known to exist today. Pop culture value, you ask? Well, Marathon is technically the only car ever built in Nashville - Nissan and Saturn are outside the city limits. Also, the building now houses Antique Archaeology, the business in the popular television show, *American Pickers*.

MAXWELL HOUSE
NW Corner of 4th Ave N & Church St

Originally located far from its current spot in Metrocenter, the Maxwell House hotel was situated on the corner of

Cherry and Spring Streets. Built by John Overton, it was the largest hotel in Nashville at the time and criticized by many who thought Nashville to be too small to warrant such a grand hotel. It was used by both Confederate and

Union armies during the Civil War and, most notably, is where Theodore Roosevelt coined the phrase "Good to the last drop" after tasting the private blend of coffee named after the hotel. Maxwell House coffee was eventually purchased by General Foods in 1928 for more than $40 million.

NATIONAL LIFE AND ACCIDENT INSURANCE BUILDING
NW Corner of 7th and Union

On this unassuming street corner once stood one of the most historically valuable locations to Nashville pop culture: the National Life and Accident Insurance Building. While the name doesn't sound all that exciting, the companies that occupied the building as well as the events that took place inside are profound.

As the building name suggests, its main occupant was the National Life and Accident Insurance Company. Their catchphrase is the famous "We Shield Millions" which, if you haven't heard before, you will no doubt hear at some point in your time in Nashville. In 1924, National Life was looking for new ways to invest some of it's money as well as promote their insurance products...and what better way to advertise than  on it's very own radio station! Thus, in this very building, in a fifth floor radio studio, the station AM 650 WSM ("We Shield Millions") was born.

When George Hay came in as a disc jockey to WSM, he brought with him an idea to create a radio show spotlighting hillbilly music. On November 25, 1925, at 8:00pm, the first "WSM Barn Dance" debuted featuring championship fiddler, Uncle Jimmy Thompson. The name of the Barn Dance was inadvertently modified on December 10, 1927, to the "Grand Ole Opry" when, after a segment on WSM featuring classical opera music, George Hay quoted, "For the past hour, we have been listening to music taken largely from Grand Opera. From now on, we will present the "Grand Ole Opry"...and the name stuck.

Due to overwhelming popularity and the need to accommodate large audiences, the Grand Ole Opry left the National Life building in 1934 and switched numerous locations before finally landing in the Ryman Auditorium from 1943 to 1974. At that point, it moved to its current location, the Grand Ole Opry House.

Not only was the Grand Ole Opry born here but it was in the WSM break room of this building in September of 1946 that, according to legend, a man unexpectedly interrupted a game of ping-pong that Fred Rose was enjoying, and told Rose that he wanted to play him some songs. Rose was so impressed by his songwriting and his performance that he signed him up immediately. That mans name was Hank Williams. History had been made.

Not to diminish the fun in legends like that but, in actuality, Hank Williams had been formally invited to Nashville after Fred Rose had already heard some of his material in the weeks prior to. Their initial meetings did, however, take place in this building and indeed history was made in a small office in the building that once stood here. There just wasn't a whole lot of ping-pong.

Last but certainly not least...and to add to Nashville's impact on the radio industry...the very first FM radio license in the United States was granted to the National Life and Accident Insurance Company by the FCC in 1941 for WSM-FM, originally known as W47NV. Unfortunately, not a whole lot of radio listeners had FM radios at the time and the FM venture eventually went off the air.

NEW ERA CLUB

4th Ave, where the Municipal Auditorium stands today

On this site once stood one of the main stops on the national R&B circuit, the New Era Club. Opened in 1939, the New Era had the same reputation as clubs like The Apollo in New York and The Regal in Chicago and would  host up-and-coming legends like Ray Charles, B.B. King, and James Brown when they toured through Nashville. It was also here that Etta James' recorded her classic live album *Etta James Rocks The House* in 1963.

SHELBY STREET BRIDGE

Shelby Ave, crossing over the Cumberland River just south of downtown

At 3,150 feet, this was once the "longest pedestrian bridge in the world" until the Poughkeepsie-Highland Railroad Bridge knocked it out of contention in 2009. After more than 100 years in service, this steel truss and concrete bridge was  considered too unsafe for vehicular passage so it was downgraded to a now-popular pedestrian walkway over the river. "One Of The Longest Pedestrian Bridges in the World" still has a respectable ring to it.

THE STANDARD

167 Rosa L Parks Blvd, Nashville
www.SmithHouseNashville.com

This Nashville icon was built in the late 1840's by the Claiborne family as a boarding house with many of Nashville's most prominent citizens at the time as residents. After serving as a Union headquarters during the Civil War in planning strategy for the Battle of Nashville, the Standard Club itself was established in the house during the 1890's and introduced Nashville's first official grand ballroom. Nashville's first bowling alley quickly followed underneath the ballroom, the decorate tin roof of which can still be viewed today. Other pop culture items include the famous fireplace mantle where President Andrew Jackson renewed his vows to Rachel still on display in the ballroom, as well as a number of secret rooms along with a tunnel under 8th Avenue rumored to have been part of the Underground Railroad. More recently, the property was featured in the Brad Paisley/Allison Krauss video for "Whiskey Lullaby".

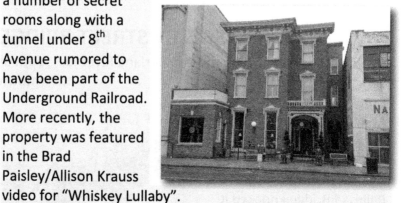

While the original Standard Club has long since moved to the Old Natchez Country Club, the new Standard Club opened in 2005 as a restored restaurant and nationally acclaimed private cigar club.

MUSIC ROW: SONY BUILDING
1400 18th Ave S.

Sony Music Nashville is quartered in a former convent and hospice. It is listed on the National Register of Historic Places due to its unique features, one of which is the stone-carving on the north end of the building that reads "Home For The Aged".

MUSIC ROW: STREET LAMPS

The original Music Row is marked with unique streetlamps up and down. Jerry Bradley worked with Mayor Briley at the time to get office owners along the Row to pay for the lamps, placing one in front of the offices that paid. Music Row has obviously expanded but if there's no street lamp, it's not the "real" Row.

MUSIC ROW: TIM MCGRAW
47 Music Sq. E

For all you Tim McGraw fans, this is the building that he originally met Mike Borchetta of Curb Records in before signing his record deal with the label.

UNIVERSITY OF NASHVILLE REMNANTS
Edgehill Avenue south of Magnolia Circle, on the left when traveling west

Inscription: These Ionic column capitals once adorned the Cumberland College building constructed in 1806 just south of downtown Nashville. Originally founded in December 1785 as Davidson Academy (the nation's 15th college), Cumberland's charter was altered in 1826, changing its name to University of Nashville. In 1875, the State Normal School was founded by the Peabody Education Fund and was affiliated with the University of Nashville until 1909 when it was incorporated as George Peabody College for Teachers. In 1914 the college moved to this campus and in 1979 merged with Vanderbilt University.

34

Peabody College, founded in 1875 as the State Normal College, was originally affiliated with the University of Nashville, which traced its roots to Davidson Academy, founded in 1785. This Plaque was displayed on the Gate Keeper's lodge, built in 1889 near the main entrance to the old "South Campus," located on Market Street (today 2nd Avenue) and home to the University of Nashville, Montgomery Bell Academy, Peabody Normal School, and, later, Vanderbilt University's Medical and Dental Departments.

THE UPPER ROOM
1908 Grand Ave
www.UpperRoom.org

This building is a museum and the home of the publication *The Upper Room*, which delivers daily non-denominational inspirations. Inside the museum, you'll find antique Bibles, letters from religious leaders from all over the world, a stunning 2-story high stained glass window, as well as the only carved wooden sculpture of the Last Supper of it's kind, standing over 17 feet tall.

ICONS

Much like the Eiffel Tower helps instantly identify Paris, or the Alamo defines San Antonio, there are a number of places around Nashville that help truly make it "Nashville". From world-famous venues like the Bluebird Cafe to "Batman" on the skyline, these are places that leave an distinct impression of the Nashville experience.

3RD AND LINDSLEY

818 3rd Ave S.
www.3rdAndLindsley.com

Since 1991, the too-good-to-be-true intimacy of 3rd & Lindsley has hosted up-and-coming major acts such as Train, Sister Hazel, The Fray, Jason Mraz, Joss Stone, Better Than Ezra, Sheryl Crow, and Kings of Leon. Patty Griffin recorded her most popular live bootleg here in 1996 and the world-renowned Wooten Brothers called 3rd & Lindsley their home on Wednesday nights for a number of years.

In 2011, the venue expanded it's size and doubled it's stage for a much more traditional setup compared to the

controversial "L" shape it had been for so many years. The old stage, marred by the scratches from amps of legendary players and drooping from the footsteps of incomparable artists, was unfortunately hauled off to the landfill.

328 PERFORMANCE HALL
328 4th Ave S

Once upon a time, there was the 328 Performance Hall just south of downtown. It did not shine, it did not sparkle. In fact, all it really was was a big room...you know the kind: flat, barely a stage riser, hard to see around the awkwardly swaying guy in front of you. However, the sound waves that filled the air here are almost too impressive to comprehend. In it's heyday, 328 held small club performances by The Melvins, The Flaming Lips, The Strokes, Sevendust, The Misfits, Megadeth, GWAR, 311, Guster, Korn, Everclear, Foo Fighters, Black Crowes, Dave Matthews, Smashing Pumpkins, Blues Traveler, and John Mayer...just to name a few. While most of the legacy is lost, a few performances still exist on YouTube. As for the building itself, a Hampton Inn now sits on the site.

BATMAN BUILDING
333 Commerce St

Easily the most notable landmark of the Nashville skyline, the professionals call it "The "AT&T Building" while the rest of us call it "The Batman Building". Seriously, it doesn't get much cooler that a building that looks like Batman! 'Nuff said.

BLUEBIRD CAFE
4104 Hillsboro Pike
www.BluebirdCafe.com

There is no greater locale for songwriters in Nashville and perhaps the world than the legendary Bluebird Café. Unassumingly set back in a low-key Green Hills strip mall, the Bluebird has been the breeding ground for songwriters since it's establishment by Amy Kurland in 1982. Kathy Mattea scored a record deal after performing at the Bluebird in 1983 and after that, songwriters flocked to be part of the scene.

The current tradition of songwriter "rounds" were born at the Bluebird when Fred Knobloch, Don Schlitz, Paul Overstreet, and Thom Schuyler performed the first writers round there, after Fred and Don devised the idea. You can now see these songwriter's rounds at essentially every venue in Nashville.

The Bluebird Café is the backdrop for the Peter Bogdonavich film, *The Thing Called Love*, starring River Phoenix, Sandra Bullock, Samantha Mathis, and Dermot Mulroney. Many of the exterior scenes were filmed right there in the parking lot as well as other Nashville locations (see Filming Locations section). This was River Phoenix's last film before his untimely death a few weeks after shooting wrapped.

Perhaps the most legendary story of the Bluebird Café is what occurred on June 6, 1987. A writer by the name of Ralph Murphy was scheduled to perform at the Bluebird for a benefit but was a no-show. A young gentleman was in the audience and offered to sit in for Ralph – he proceeded onstage and sang "If Tomorrow Never Comes".

His name was Garth Brooks. It so happened that a representative from Capitol Records was in the audience (to see Ralph Murphy, ironically), went up to Garth and told him to come by the label the next day. The rest is history.

Another huge discovery at the Bluebird happened when Scott Borchetta saw a 14-year-old Taylor Swift perform at the Bluebird. Borchetta eventually signed her to his new label, Big Machine records.

Today, the Bluebird is the screening area for nearly every song that you hear hit the airwaves – veteran writers can be heard during the Late Shows while aspiring up-and-comers introduce their talents during the Early Shows. It also hosts the Sunday Writers Nights as well as an Open Mic on Monday nights. See www.BluebirdCafe.com for more information.

BRIDGESTONE ARENA
501 Broadway

Bridgestone Arena has had too many names to mention since opening in 1996: the Sommet Center, the Gaylord Entertainment Center or "GEC" for short, the Nashville Arena. Located on the southwest corner of Broadway and 5th, it was built at an angle, facing toward the Ryman Auditorium as a direct tribute to the greatest of all music venues.

Bridgestone Arena is the largest indoor venue in middle Tennessee, holding nearly 20,000 fans, and is the official home of the Nashville Predators hockey team. In addition to hockey, it has held rodeos, figure skating events, musical tours, basketball tournaments, WWE, gymnastics, numerous CMA Awards, and yep, even

New Kids On The Block. In December of 2010, Garth Brooks held unprecedented 9 sold-out shows over 6 days and raised over $1,000,000 to help benefit flood relief from the Nashville flood earlier that year. You can also see LeAnn Rimes seductively enjoying the curves of the arena in her video for "How Do I Live".

BROKEN SPOKE CAFE
1412 Brick Church Pike

For over a decade, the Broken Spoke Saloon and Songwriter's Café, located inside the Ramada Inn, was one of the more popular venues among the Nashville songwriting community. Their writer's nights were as packed as any in town, right up there with the Bluebird and Douglas Corner, if not even more popular. The Broken Spoke had a legacy of legendary writers and artists breaking out their then-new and now-classic songs to a crowd of regulars. Just mentioning it to a tenured writer will bring about a flash of nostalgia and usually ends in the question of "Man, whatever happened to the Broken Spoke?!"

While the doors closed to songwriter rounds in 2010, the stage still stands, the façade of the Old West is freshly painted, and the room can be rented for private events, if so desired. It's definitely worth a sneak-in to get a peek and to see if

you can still feel the energy that once was.

COURTYARD NASHVILLE DOWNTOWN

170 4th Ave N

This somewhat unknown Nashville icon, the current Courtyard Nashville Downtown property, on the edge of Printers Alley, has some amazing history that might be missed on a casual stroll by through downtown. Opened in 1904 and with a towering 12 stories, the building was Nashville first skyscraper, and remained the tallest in Nashville for over five years. One of the initial tenants was the Third National Bank, an institution that managed to weather the Great Depression from its headquarters at this location, as well as finance the Grand Ole Opry in their more dire times.

A fascinating piece of history of this building is the story of a man named Herman W. Lay, who got a loan from that very same bank on this property in 1938 to start his potato chip and snack company: Lay's Potato Chips. Years later, the Frito Company merged with H.W. Lay and became "Frito-Lay, Inc." (later merging with PepsiCo), which, according to their website, accounts for 59% of the U.S. snack chip industry.

Another notable event here is it being the location for Nashville's first FM radio station, W47NV. Today, the building is an Historic Landmark registered by the Nashville Historic Society.

43

DIAMOND ANTENNA
I-65 and Concord Rd

The so-called "diamond antenna" is the largest Blaw-Knox dual cantilevered antenna of it's kind. Broadcasting WSM 650AM, the station began operation October 5, 1932, the anniversary of it's founding in 1925 by the National Life and Accident Insurance Company of Nashville. WSM-AM operates on a clear channel frequency of 650 kilohertz with power of 50,000 watts, making it one of the nation's strongest signals, reaching most of the country with the Grand Ole Opry, which it has continued to broadcast on a

regular basis. The tower was originally 878 feet high and was the tallest radio tower in the U.S. at the time of its erection (it was subsequently shortened to 808 feet to eliminate signal loss at the 120 miles range). It remains the largest Blaw-Knox diamond tower, sitting on a large porcelain insulator and held vertical by eight insulated steel cables.

DOUGLAS CORNER

2106 8th Ave S.

www.DouglasCorner.com

Since 1987, Douglas Corner Café has been known as a songwriter's "Home Away From Home" and is still one of the most popular songwriter venues in Nashville, where  the likes of Jon Bon Jovi, Neil Diamond, Bruce Hornsby, Bela Fleck, George Strait, Keith Urban (who used to live around the corner), Mac Davis, Blake Shelton, and Alan Jackson have all been seen and have performed unforgettable intimate shows.

Trisha Yearwood was "discovered" here after playing here with Pat Alger's band, the Algerians. Garth Brooks was playing darts in the back when he heard the song "Wolves" for the first time. Tony Arata performed "The Dance" for the first time ever in Douglas Corner. And Keith Whitley used Douglas Corner as the backdrop for his final video, "I'm No Stranger To The Rain".

One item of note is the shoe hanging on the wall behind the bar. According to owner, Mervin Louque, the story goes that back in 1987, Tony Arata and Scott Miller barely had a nickel to their name but happened to find this shoe in the middle of the road. They decided their best bet was to take this shoe to Mervin at Douglas Corner and use it to negotiate their cover charge and a few beers at the bar. Mervin saw that it was a size 11...so he gave them $11 of credit, mainly for their creativity and for giving him a good laugh. The shoe hung for awhile behind the bar as a joke until Tony was nominated for a Grammy for "The Dance", at which point,

Mervin and Scott overnighted the shoe to Tony in New York on a whim. This shoe actually attended the Grammy's with Tony Arata that year and was then returned to its rightful position behind the Douglas Corner bar.

Douglas Corner also provides state-of-the-art onsite audio and video production (and mobile, if needed) for artists and showcases. Visit www.DouglasCorner.com for more info.

DRAKE MOTEL
420 Murfreesboro Pike

The Drake Motel, just southeast of downtown, is one of those places that you feel like you've seen before but you just didn't know you saw it. The motto on the sign famously says "Stay where the stars stay!", which may have been true at one time. If fact, according to the photos in the lobby, if one has a signature on it, then apparently that celebrity stayed at the motel. This would impressively include Elvis, Johnny Cash, and even Sandra Bullock. These days, though, the Drake seems content with its historical legacy and more likely provides low cost lodging for "stars-that-lost-their-record-deal-and-just-got-evicted".

46

The Drake Motel has been featured in many film and TV productions. Most famously, it was the motel where Samantha Mathis and Sandra Bullock stayed in the cult-classic "The Thing Called Love". Samantha Mathis' initial "Disco Room" is #107 (#108 in the movie) and the motel has commemorated this with a plaque on the door that appropriately states "Thing Called Love Room".

Sandra Bullock's room is #127 but was built on a California soundstage. Neither room is still furnished as it was for the movie.

A number of music videos have featured the Drake Motel. Collin Raye stood on the 2nd floor stairwell landing of the building directly northwest of the Drake in the video for "Little Rock". Jason Aldean used to Drake in the video for "The Truth". Darryl Worley filmed his video for "Nothin' But A Love Thang" at the Drake. Also, the movie "Songbird" with Dolly Parton and Billy Dean was set at the motel.

ERNEST TUBB RECORD SHOP

417 Broadway
www.ETRecordShop.com

Ernest Tubb opened his record shop in 1947 as a mail-order business to provide fans with the ability to order records and albums that might be unavailable in their local areas. The popularity of his mail-order business, along with his catchy commercials on the Opry, led to the opening of this location in 1951 as well

as the Midnight Jamboree that happens at the store every Saturday night and is still broadcast on 650-AM WSM after 60 years (although it is now broadcast from the Texas Troubadour Theater by Opryland).

The Ernest Tubb Record Shop prides itself on having access and inventory of classic records that customers simply can't get back home, as well as vinyl options of current artists. Visitors to one of the oldest remaining record stores in the world – and easily the most famous – can shop for their favorite Country music, view Pete Drake's famous "Talking Guitar", and will easily recognize the stage in the back from the classic film *Coal Miner's Daughter*.

EXIT/IN

2208 Elliston Place
www.ExitIn.com

Nashville's version of Hollywood's Whisky A-Go-Go, the Exit/In has seen the likes of Bruce Springsteen, Billy Joel, Elton John, Tom Petty, The Police, REM, Barry Manilow, Lyle Lovett, and even Kris Kristofferson, amongst many, many others...most of them long before they were ever household names. A wall-of-fame is on display inside (the outside one is a very recent, more touristy addition) and contains more jaw-dropping names that will make any visitor wish they could have been there if they weren't. It was also heavily featured in Robert Altman's epic film, *Nashville.*

And for you performers, the Exit/In has the most consistent sound that this author has heard in Nashville, just in case you're looking to book your next gig.

FONTANEL

4225 Whites Creek Pike, Whites Creek, TN
www.fontanelmansion.com

This impressive property is the former home of Barbara Mandrell and has become a prime Nashville destination for locals and tourists alike. As the cities only country music mansion tour AND as what once was the largest log home in America, the Fontanel mansion experience consists of a 27,000 square foot house (3 stories, 20 rooms, 13 bathrooms, 5 fireplaces, 2 kitchens, and an indoor pool), an event plaza with a gift shop and convention halls, a distillery, the very tasty Café Fontanella, the Woods at Fontanel amphitheater, and miles of hiking trails all nestled on a 136 acres of surrounding land. The mansion is currently owned by Dale Morris and Marc Oswald, two of Nashville's powerhouse managers of artists like Alabama, Big & Rich, and Kenny Chesney. Tours are available 7 days a week.

GARTH BROOKS

Alright, here's the deal. This book started out because I'm a Garth Brooks fanatic. I grew up fascinated by the stories of him coming to town with his old band, working at Cowtown Boots in Rivergate, sealing his record deal at the Bluebird Café, his famous driveway gate...the list goes on. As a result, I have accumulated a bit of Garth history over the years and I love to tell it to people. So in honor of biggest selling solo artist in Country Music history – and the man that made it more popular than ever – Mr. Brooks gets his own section. If you're not a fan, feel free to skip to the next section. But if you are, this is some must-see stuff!

GARTH BROOKS
Tennessee Home
1250 Genelle Dr

Once the governor's mansion, this property was renovated in the early 1990's to the specifications of the most popular Country Music artist in history, Garth Brooks. The house, which Garth proposed to convert into a museum once his Oklahoma residence was completed (neighbors rejected the proposal), is nice and all...but the most impressive feature here is the barn which has in indoor riding arena, basketball court, and other amenities.

Unfortunately, the main gate is all that is really visible but it's worth getting a picture in front of just to say you were there.

GARTH BROOKS
First Home Rented
104 Forrest Meadows Ct, Hendersonville, TN

When Garth first arrived in town, he and Sandy Brooks lived in this duplex in Hendersonville.

GARTH BROOKS
Cowtown Boots
2021 Gallatin Pike #208

Just down the main drag is Rivergate Mall, where he famously sold boots at Cowtown Boots – the location of the boot store is now partially occupied by a sushi restaurant.

Joe Calcaterra III, who was opening the store, remembers: "I was in a hurry to get the store ready for the opening. Garth walks in on a Saturday to interview for the Store Manager position. I told him that I would know by that afternoon who I would hire. He said 'I don't mind waiting' and then stuck around for 7 hours, helping me get the store ready...and he wasn't even hired yet! Of course, he was hired, though."

GARTH BROOKS
1705 Warfield Dr

If the whole "Garth Brooks Phenomenon" could be pinpointed to one location in Nashville, it would be this house. Kent Blazy owned this house and maintained a home studio in it where he would hire demo singers such as Garth, Trisha Yearwood, Joe Diffie, Martina McBride, Faith Hill, Rob Crosby, and Billy Dean.

Bob Doyle accompanied Garth to a demo session here one day in 1987 and mentioned that Garth did some songwriting as well.

Kent and Garth got together on February 1, 1988 to work on a song of which Garth had the 2nd Verse and the Chorus. It was called "If Tomorrow Never Comes" and would be Garth's first #1 record and begin the catapult to superstardom. Garth, Kent, and their co-writers wrote a number of hits here, including:

If Tomorrow Never Comes
How You Ever Gonna Know
Cold Shoulder
Somewhere Other Than The Night

This is also the house where Kent introduced Garth Brooks and Trisha Yearwood to each other. Kent had been prodding Garth to meet a female vocalist he was working with so he arranged for them sing on a duet he was recording, forcing them to cross paths.

Blazy: "I still drive past that house and just remember the magic and being at the start of the whirlwind...not even being aware of how it was taking off but then becoming aware of: 'Ok, this is something I need to be cognitive of'."

GARTH BROOKS
Jack's Tracks
1308 16th Ave S

Anytime you hear a Garth song, unless it was live, it was recorded in this studio with the band playing live to analog a few feet away from Brooks at a simple burlap and foam-covered vocal baffle. Garth even wrote a number of his hits here, such as "Thunder Rolls", "Unanswered Prayers", "What She's Doing Now", "That Summer", and "Like We Never Had A Broken Heart". Tony Arata wrote the Chris Gaines song, "That's The Way I Remember It" here, as well. For more info, see the "STUDIOS" section.

GARTH BROOKS
1026 Overton Lea

Kent Blazy and Co. wrote a number of Garth hits such as "Ain't Goin' Down", "She's Gonna Make It", "Cowboys & Angels", and "It's Midnight Cinderella" at this house, as well as Diamond Rio's "That's What I Get For Loving You", and Chris LeDoux's "Slow Down" on the back patio.

GARTH BROOKS
House Used In Video For "If Tomorrow Never Comes"
3590 Brick Church Pike

Technically, this address is just the very private access road to the property so best not to approach unless you live there. Your best view is take I-24 westbound during the winter, look to your right at the blue "Food – Exit 40" sign, and you'll be able to see the house clearly through the trees on the right hand side.

GAYLORD OPRYLAND HOTEL AND RESORT

2800 Opryland Dr.
www.GaylordOpryland.com

The Gaylord Opryland Hotel and Resort in Nashville is the largest non-casino resort in America. Located on a sprawling nine-acre self-sufficient complex, the Opryland Hotel is lavish in every detail, boasting gorgeous Vegas-style waterfalls, a

riverboat ride through tropical terrain, fine dining, live music in a variety of well-placed bars, as well as over 600,000 feet of convention space. During the holidays, thousands flock to see Opryland decorated and it's world-class display of lights.

The hotel was devastated by the May 2010 flooding, which caused $225 million in damage to the hotel alone, shut down operations for 6 months, and required the lay-off of 1,700 employees. Astounding photos of the interior of the Opryland Hotel under more than 10 feet of water appear to be the aftermath of a Tahitian tsunami.

The hotel reopened in September of 2010, renovated and more majestic than ever. No trip to Nashville is complete without a walk through the hotel, a river ride, and a peek into the current location of the 650-AM WSM studios in the Magnolia wing.

HATCH SHOW PRINT
224 5th Ave S

Hatch Show Print has been providing one of the most recognizable poster designs since 1875, when Wisconsin printer, Rev. William T. Hatch moved his family to Nashville. He taught his two sons, Charles and Herbert, the printing business and upon his death in 1879, they opened the first Hatch print shop at 22 North Cherry St. Initially, they printed handbills, vaudeville promotions, and circus flyers. Word of their eye-catching designs got around, though, and since the 1930's, Hatch Show has been providing the posters for most Grand Ole Opry performers, as well as collectible Ryman prints (like Coldplay, Springsteen, and Counting Crows) and other local venues.

The posters are still printed one at a time through a process that involves hand-carved wooden lettering blocks, hand-inked rollers, and progressing each sheet through the 4-color pressing. The popular consensus is that what makes the posters so recognizable are the unique Hatch fonts that contrast perfectly with and against each other. The Country Music Hall Of Fame website says it best: "The Hatch brothers got the look right. Here was the simplicity, the effortless balance between type size and style, vertical and horizontal layout. Here, too, was the distinct whiff of American history, southern culture, and entertainment."

After over 125 years and 8 location changes, Hatch Show Print is now adjacent to the Country Music Hall of Fame and

Omni Hotel, near the heart of downtown. 20,000 visitors pop into the store every year – don't be afraid to stop in and get a collectible print that will hang proudly on any wall.

HERMITAGE HOTEL
231 6th Ave N
www.TheHermitageHotel.com

In the early 1900's, competition was fierce among hotels to be the grandest and most luxurious hotel. The Maxwell House, the Tulane, the Duncan hotels all battled for these honors. But only one still stands: the Hermitage Hotel.

A 5-Star hotel since 2004, The Hermitage Hotel has seen more than it's fair share of U.S. Presidents (John F. Kennedy, Bill Clinton, Richard Nixon), movie stars (Tom Cruise, Clint Eastwood, Bette Midler), and A-list celebrities (Oprah, Steven Spielberg, George Lucas). Al Capone stayed here while traveling the Dixie Highway between Chicago and St.

Petersburg, Florida to "do business". Al Jolson and big band acts of the day such as Doris Day and Benny Goodman were regulars.

Francis Craig's Orchestra was a staple from the northeast corner of the Oak Bar and Grill Room from 1929 to 1949. It was during this time that Craig introduced a woman by the name of Frances Rose Shore in that very room. She later changed her first name to "Dinah". While initially widely known for writing the Vanderbilt fight song "Dynamite", Craig wrote the #1 classic, "Near You", on a Grill Room menu while sitting at the bar of the restaurant. "Near You" was #1 on the Billboard charts for 17 consecutive weeks, in the Top 10 for 25, and was adopted by Milton Berle as his theme song.

In 1941, Gene Autry checked into the hotel...along with his horse, Champion, who received full care in his own private suite. The room had been fitted with canvas covering to make it "horse friendly" and hotel bellman, Horace Bernstein, was given the duty of caring for Champion during his stay. Bernstein would attend to Champion's water and walk him in Memorial Square daily. When they checked out, Autry and Champion tipped Bernstein a hefty $100 when 25 cents would have been appropriate. The hotel has been pet-friendly ever since.

Perhaps one of the most iconic guests of the Hermitage was Minnesota Fats, the world's greatest billiards player. Fats permanently moved into the Hermitage Hotel in 1985 at the age of 72 and stayed for 8 years. He was the self-proclaimed Hermitage Hotel's "Ambassador of Nashville", entertaining people for hours with his hustling and trick shots on a $3,200 table given to him by the hotel. Players at these games included the likes of Bono and Johnny Cash.

No doubt, the most notorious aspect of the Hermitage Hotel is its famous green and black Art deco men's room. Designed in the 1940's by hotel manager William Caldwell, this bathroom has won  awards for "Best Restroom In America" and is an easy winner for the unofficial "Men's Room Seen By Most Women" award. Countless photo shoots, music videos, and showcases have featured the Hermitage Hotel men's room...go ahead, take a peek! It's OK, ladies...

JACK DANIELS DISTILLERY

182 Lynchburg Hwy, Lyrchburg TN 37352
www.JackDaniels.com

Hidden in the hills of south central Tennessee is one of the most world-renowned products to come out of the south: the original Jack Daniels distillery, which has made the town of "Lynchburg" a household name amongst whiskey aficionados. The most ironic fact of this location is that, although Jack Daniels is perhaps the most recognizable whiskey in the world, it's original facility and headquarters is located in a gosh-darn *dry county*, of all places. On a standard tour, you'll get the story of Mr. Daniels, hear of the foundation of the company, and get to see the exact spring where Jack drew water for the first sips of his empire (this authors favorite part)...but there will be no tasting, unfortunately (this authors not-so-favorite part). Fear not, though - sampling is now available on an upgraded tour. And while the distillery is the main draw of the area, make sure to take in the town of Lynchburg as well, which has it's own charm and is worth the trip itself.

KING OF THE ROAD MOTEL

211 N. First St

Let's face it, the only desirable trait of this hotel anymore is its legacy...but sometimes that, along with a little character, is all a building needs to grab your attention. Built by Roger Miller, the "King Of The Road Motel" (currently a less-than-glamorous Days Inn) is famous for its guitar-shaped swimming pool as well as for a nightclub that used to sit atop the building. Although the nightclub is long gone and conference space now fills the spot, it is not forgotten that Ronnie Milsap used to rock the living daylights out of this rooftop room, attracting the attention of Jerry Bradley at RCA who eventually signed him.

DID YOU KNOW:
MINNIE PEARL – COUNTRY MUSIC HALL OF FAME PLAQUE

When you walk through the Country Music Hall of Fame, take special note to look at Minnie Pearl's plaque in the rotunda. You might notice that it's a little bit different than the other plaques in that there's no "date of death" for Minnie Pearl. Sarah Ophelia Conner, Minnie's creator and mortal embodiment, said that while she herself might leave this world, "Minnie Pearl" would live forever...and therefore, there is only a date of birth for Minnie on the plaque.

MUSICIAN'S HALL OF FAME
401 Gay Street, Nashville, in the Municipal Auditorium
www.MusiciansHallOfFame.com

One of the hidden gems of Nashville, The Musicians Hall of Fame & Museum honors all musicians regardless of genre or instrument. The MHOF timeline starts with the beginning of recorded music and inductees are nominated by current members of the American Federation of Musicians, as well as other music industry professionals. The artifacts,

61

instruments, and stories that are on display will leave any visitor feeling like they're in the presence of greatness and true history. Their Grammy Gallery is truly remarkable, as are their tributes to the Wrecking Crew, the Swampers, Jimi Hendrix, and the Funk Brothers. This stop is definitely worth the trip.

PARTHENON

Centennial Park, 2600 West End Avenue

One of the most recognizable landmarks in all of Nashville is this full-scale reproduction of the Athenian temple, the Parthenon. Built in 1897 in support of Nashville's proclamation of being the "Athens Of The South" as well as a highlight for the 1900 Centennial Celebration, it became permanent after restoration in 1931 and houses the largest indoor sculpture in the Western World, Athena, a 42-foot magnificent statue gilded in 23.75 carat Italian gold leaf.

It has been featured in a number of films like *Percy Jackson & the Olympians*, and the Robert Altman classic, *Nashville*.

Inscribed: The Nashville Parthenon was built on this site as the centerpiece of the Tennessee Centennial Exposition of 1897. The original full-scale replica was intended as a temporary exhibit structure and was constructed of brick, wood and plaster. The building quickly endeared itself to all Nashvillans who protested plans for the building's demolition at the close of the Centennial Celebration. The original building stood until 1921 at which time the City of Nashville began the reconstruction of the worn structure— this time with permanent materials. This building, the result of those efforts, was completed in 1931.

The Parthenon was listed in the National Register of Historic Places on February 23, 1972.

PUB OF LOVE
123 12th Ave N.

Big Kenny and John Rich put the now-closed Pub Of Love on the pop culture map when, in October of 2001, they got together here with a few friends and start jamming with no discrimination on style or genre. Thus was formed the Muzik Mafia who called this their home for a year and a half before outgrowing the place with their ever-increasing fan base. Products of the Muzik Mafia include Big & Rich, Gretchen Wilson, James Otto, Cowboy Troy, and Two-Foot Fred, amongst others.

NOT IN NASHVILLE:
SEE ROCK CITY!

Although not technically a "Nashville-only" site, the legacy of the "See Rock City!" barns throughout the south originated not too far away. According to Rock City itself: "Since Rock

City Gardens was off the beaten path, Garnet Carter had to devise a way to get the public up the mountain to see this unique attraction. In 1936, he dreamed up a new kind of road sign, one that would ultimately become as famous as Rock City itself. Summoning a young painter named Clark Byers, he told him of his plan to paint an advertising message on the roofs of barns alongside major highways. By the 1950's, Garnet's message was painting on over 800 roofs from Michigan to Texas to Florida. Journalists began calling Clark and his helpers the "Barnyard Rembrants," and vacationers by the thousands heeded the call to "See Rock City". Garnet died in 1954 and Clark died in 2004. Garnet's ideas and Clark's hard work are still evident along many U.S. highways and are much loved pieces of Americana."

RYMAN AUDITORIUM
116 5th Ave N
www.Ryman.com

The "Mother Church Of Country Music" was built by Reverend Sam Jones and Thomas Ryman in 1888 to be used as the Union Gospel Tabernacle. It was primarily the gathering place for Reverend Jones' large congregation but also began to function as a public forum for entertainment events such as operas, theater, rodeos, and even livestock auctions. In 1897, the Confederate Veterans Association decided to hold their annual event at the Ryman but needed more room so they contributed funds to have the balcony constructed, therefore earning it the name "Confederate Gallery" (which is not always widely accepted by artists performing there – there is a cover that is sometimes draped over the sign in case any of them decide that they disagree with the historical significance). The original Gallery wrapped nearly entirely around the pulpit (now backstage) but the wings were removed during later renovations.

Countless amazing moments have happened in the Ryman but we'll tackle a few key ones here. One of the most historically defining events in music happened at the Ryman when Bill Monroe, along with Earl Scruggs, Lester Flatt, Chubby Wise, and Cedric Rainwater, introduced the East Tennessee style of what they called "Bluegrass" to the Opry audience in 1945, making it the undisputed "Birthplace of Bluegrass".

Roy Rogers' horse, Trigger, has even graced the stage, as has a kid named Elvis in a single, forgettable appearance. The story goes that Elvis, quickly becoming a musical icon, had been invited to audition for the Opry. He excitedly arrived and performed his rendition of "Blue Moon of Kentucky". As he was leaving, the stage manager asked Elvis what he did before he started singing, to which Elvis replied, "I used to drive a truck!" The stage manager responded, "Well, after hearing that song, son, I suggest you start looking for the keys." Elvis never performed at the Ryman again.

It was also on this stage that Hank Williams made his Grand Ole Opry debut, where he was cheered on for an unbelievable *seven* encores of "Lovesick Blues". Johnny Cash kicked out the stage lights in an infamous (and stoned) bout of anger with his microphone stand and was subsequently banned from the Ryman stage. Ironically, the Ryman later became home to the Johnny Cash Show from 1969 to 1971.

Minnie Pearl had a historic moment on the Ryman stage with a new hat she had just bought...the price tag inadvertently fell out from it's hiding spot in the flowers in the band and dangled for the very first time. The Everly Brothers were discovered after performing outside the backstage door for a number of weeks before Chet Atkins finally invited them to play during his slot on the Opry. Even rock star, Ryan Adams, had an infamous meltdown onstage here when a fan spitefully requested "Summer Of '69". Adams, having heard the Bryan Adams joke one too many times at that point, took $35 from his own wallet, threw it at the fan, and had him escorted out.

The Ryman also has its share of ghosts, as any historical building should have: legend has it that Hank can be seen turning around corners at the far end of the hall and that Patsy's heels still walk the halls at night. There is also the persistent sighting of a Confederate Soldier sitting in the Gallery section 13 when there is not another soul in the building. The scariest event to haunt the Ryman, though, is that of Ashlee Simpson being allowed to perform on the coveted stage in 2005.

Although it is not the original home, the Ryman Auditorium was home to the Grand Ole Opry from 1943 until 1974, when the Opry moved across the river to the new Grand Ole Opry House, although it returns to the Ryman every November for an annual homecoming. A large circle of the original stage was cut from the rear right section (they assumed that most of the footfalls had crossed that spot) and installed into the stage of the Opry House.

The Ryman was closed from 1974 until 1994 and fell into extreme disrepair after the departure of the Opry. Nashville owes a debt of gratitude to Emmylou Harris who, in the early 1990's, performed a series of shows and released 1992's *At The Ryman* which regenerated interest in the venue and enabled it's renovation.

Today, you can tour the Ryman, stand on the stage, sing into the microphone, record your own song in the recording booth that has been installed into the original box office, sit in the original pews, find out about the time capsule underneath the stage, and enjoy the magic of the most incredible venue on the planet. Make sure you take the extended tour.

TOOTSIE'S ORCHID LOUNGE
422 Broadway
www.Tootsies.net

Tootsie's Orchid Lounge has been the most consistent landmark on lower Broadway for over 50 years. The bright purple (orchid) façade and its classic, instantly recognizable "World Famous" sign has made its mark as it has enticed countless singers, songwriters, tourists, and even Opry legends through its doors.

Tootsie's was opened as "Mom's" by "Tootsie" Ross but spent most of its heyday under the ownership of Big Jeff Bess and his wife, Hattie "Tootsie" Bess. The orchid exterior was more of an accident when a painter decided to mix the paint that he had leftover from the interior job so that he'd have enough for the exterior.

The music in Tootsie's began as jam sessions between the players of Opry bands, who would hang out in the "industry only" back room and play (and drink) together after their Opry sets. Rumor has it that a fair share of these drinking sessions took place in between their Opry sets resulting in a 2nd set that was usually a tad bit looser than the first. After all, it was only 17 steps from the backstage door of the Ryman to the back door of Tootsie's - and then 34 back, according to Willie. It was not uncommon on any given night to see the likes of Patsy Cline, Faron Young, or Webb Pierce hanging out...or later on, Willie Nelson, Kris Kristofferson, Jimmy Dean and Harlan Howard together. And for any songwriter that was a little low on cash, Tootsie herself would run them an on-going tab and might even slip a few bucks in their pocket when she could.

The list of major artists who have performed at Tootsie's is pretty much this: everyone. Whether they were fresh off the bus or even a little more established, there probably aren't too many singers or songwriters who have not graced one of Tootsie's stages. Terri Clark was discovered here..."Red Solo Cup" got it's finishing touches in this bar...Roger Miller met Buddy Killen and got his first publishing deal here...Willie Nelson even lived in the apartment above the bar for a while.

Speaking of Willie, when you visit, make sure you stop by the "VIP" booth at the very front of the bar...the bay window one to the left of the front door. Sit down and take a deep breath and take in the air of the atmosphere. Order a beer and let your hands tell the story of the scars on the wood table. Contemplate that you're actually sitting in the spot where Willie pitched the future Patsy Cline iconic classic "Crazy" to her husband, Charlie Dick, and sold his first song in Nashville. Proceed to love Tootsie's.

TWITTY CITY

1 Music Village Blvd, Hendersonville
www.TrinityMusicCity.com

The legendary Conway Twitty built this entertainment complex and lived here until his death in 1993. It was a popular Nashville tourist spot throughout the 80's, an intimate concert venue (think "Vince Gill playing guitar for Steve Wariner" type of shows) and was renowned for its display of Christmas lights.

Today, Twitty City has been converted into a Christian Music venue and is operated by the Trinity Broadcasting Network. Tours of the mansion and grounds are still in operation – and they're free!

WILDHORSE SALOON

120 2nd Ave N
www.wildhorsesaloon.com

The Wildhorse Saloon is easily one of Nashville's most visited tourist and live music destinations. Boasting over 10 million bottles of beer sold annually, 50,000 t-shirts, and a number of other impressive benchmarks, the Wildhorse is a remodeled 66,000 square foot warehouse that now contains one of Nashville's largest dance floors and 3 levels to view the always bustling entertainment stage. Die-hard country music fans will recognize the club as the location for the appropriately named *Wildhorse Saloon Dance Show* on TNN during the line-dancing craze of the mid-90's. These days, the Wildhorse is a premiere live music (and line-dancing) venue, hosting limited engagement acts as well as appearing as the backdrop for American Idol auditions, music videos, and some 4,000 other television features.

INFAMY

Nashville ain't all drinking songs and cowboy hats, boys and girls. It's seen it's fair share of tragedy throughout the years. For a taste of the dark side of pop culture, here are a few items that have made the headlines over the years.

DOTTIE WEST CRASH SITE
Opryland Exit on Briley Pkwy

On August 30, 1991, Dottie West was late to her appearance on the Grand Ole Opry that night due to her car breaking down on Harding Road. Her neighbor, George Thackston, saw her on the side of the road and offered to drive her to the Opry House. The 81-year old Thackston was allegedly encouraged to  speed by West so she could make her show on time...to which he obliged and then proceeded to lose control of the vehicle as he was exiting off of Briley Parkway onto the Opryland Exit.

Witnesses say the car flew 75 feet in the air before hitting the center exit divider. West was not actually killed in the crash but she did suffer fatal internal injuries, which ultimately claimed her life on September 4th. Thackston survived and was controversially sentenced to nearly a year of probation for Reckless Endangerment, despite an alcohol test result of .08 at the time of the accident.

ERIN ANDREWS PEEPHOLE

Marriott Nashville at Vanderbilt
2555 West End Ave, room #1051

It was in this hotel on September 4, 2008 that Erin Andrews was secretly videotaped through her hotel room #1051 peephole by stalker, Michael David Barrett. After the hotel had booked him into a room directly adjacent to hers, Barrett altered the peephole of her hotel room with a hacksaw and set up a camera, capturing several videos of her sans clothing. After the footage went viral on the internet, Andrews sued a number of defendants, including the hotel, for $10 million.

GEORGE JONES CRASH SITE

Creek bridge at approx. 4425 Murfreesboro Rd, Franklin TN

On March 6, 1999, Country legend George Jones made worldwide headlines when he lost control of his Lexus SUV on this stretch of Highway 96, between Franklin and Murfreesboro, and smashed into the concrete railing of this bridge crossing Mayes Creek. Jones had been talking to his stepdaughter on his cell phone at the time of the crash and had apparently not been wearing his seatbelt, causing a collapsed lung  and internal bleeding with the impact. Jones eventually recovered just fine after a stint in critical condition at Vanderbilt Medical Center and went on to record several more albums, as well as allow for many more "Watch out - Jones is behind the wheel again!" jokes.

HOLLY BOBO

House – 681 Swan Johnson Rd, Darden TN
Remains found – County Corner Rd, ¾ of a mile west of Holladay Rd, behind cell tower

On April 30, 2011, nursing student Holly Bobo was last seen by her brother arguing with a man in camouflage (whom he thought was her boyfriend) and then walking with him into the woods behind their parent's house at 681 Swan Johnson Rd in Darden, TN. Neighbors reported screams and a pool of blood was found near Holly's car, prompting one of the most high profile searches in middle Tennessee history. Her cell phone was quickly recovered a few miles away off of nearby Hwy 69 and a lunch box believing to be hers was also found in a creek bed...but there were no signs of Holly.

Three years passed with no major breaks in the case until ginseng hunters stumbled upon a troubling find off of County Corner Rd: partial remains that were eventually identified as Holly Bobo. The area had been previously searched without finding a trace, leading investigators to believe the body had been moved there after initial searches. In March of 2014, a local man, Zachary Adams, was arrested on unrelated assault charges and after police searched his home (at 235 Adams Ln), charged him (and a number of accomplices) in the kidnapping and murder of Holly. Adams had allegedly stalked her for as long as a year prior to her disappearance and, in a stranger twist, was a student of Holly's mother in 4th grade. As of this printing, Adams awaits trial.

JIM REEVES CRASH SITE

I-65 & Harding area, just northeast of junction of Baxter Ln and Franklin Pike Circle.

Jim Reeves plane crashed in these woods during a storm on the evening of July 31, 1964. Reeves was piloting the plane that he and his manager/piano player, Dean Manuel, were traveling in from Arkansas after a business trip. The last contact from Reeves was to the airport tower saying that he was experiencing severe weather. After the plane would not respond to further requests from the tower – and never arriving at the airport – a search party was organized, consisting of 700 searchers that included Chet Atkins, Ernest Tubb, Eddy Arnold, and even Stonewall Jackson. In an eerie twist, Marty Robbins reported hearing the whine of an engine and then a crash that night near his home, which was very close to the wreckage site. The crash was not located until Sunday afternoon, nearly two full days later in a dense growth of forest.

The actual site is difficult to pinpoint these days. It's on private property and has significantly grown over in the years since the crash. The wreckage was carted away, the crater filled in, and any signs of the site have all disappeared. No marker marks the spot.

JOHN RICH'S "MT. RICHMORE"
3432 Love Circle

This monolith has been the subject of contention since it was built back in 2010. Dubbed "Mt. Richmore", this is John Rich's version of Graceland, sitting high atop Love Circle and lowering property values as we speak. The house is 73-feet high, 11,000 square feet, has a basement parking garage, a fully-stocked bar on every level, and enough security

amenities to put even the most paranoid songwriter at ease.

Security floodlights shine 24 hours a day, blinding neighbors and blocking any semblance of a Nashville skyline view that they paid top-dollar for. The sign posted on the giant perimeter wall states that trespassers will "be shot"...but it doesn't say anything at all about eggs.

NOT IN NASHVILLE:
KKK FOUNDING
205 W Madison St
Pulaski, TN

In a darker moment of Tennessee, the infamous Ku Klux Klan was founded in this building, once a barber shop, in 1865 by a few Confederate veterans out to hinder the progressing rights of African Americans. The group, led by their first grand master, Nathan Bedford Forrest, used violence, property destruction, and murder against blacks and Republicans to influence elections and reinforce their agenda. Forrest initially tried to disband the KKK in 1869 after their violence had become too excessive but the Klan continued without him. President Grant ultimately passed a Congressional Act to use military force to eradicate the group, declaring it unconstitutional and causing the initial activity to subside. However, Klan activity has continued in the South over the past century and pockets of activism will still unfortunately make headlines today.

MARCIA TRIMBLE - HOME
4009 Copeland Drive

One of the most infamous and tragic cases in Nashville history is that of the disappearance of 9-year-old Marcia

Trimble. Marcia's family lived at this location (the previous house was torn down and rebuilt) at the time when she vanished while delivering Girl Scout Cookies on February 25, 1975. For more than a month, there was no sign, no suspect, and no leads as to what happened to Marcia.

MARCIA TRIMBLE – FOUND
4007 Estes Road

On Easter Sunday, 1975, Marcia Trimble's body was discovered in a garage that used to stand in the driveway of this house. Over a month had passed since her

disappearance but the body was still relatively well preserved. Investigation showed that Trimble had been killed in the garage after being sexually

77

assaulted and her body had been stashed under a wading pool and covered with a shower curtain. Cookies were found scattered all around her body.

For over 30 years, there were no definitive leads in the case...it wasn't until DNA testing technology advanced to the point where investigators could match the deteriorated DNA from Marcia's body to a suspect. In this case, that match pointed to Jerome Sydney Barrett, a convicted rapist who by the time of his arrest in 2007, was 60-years-old. Barrett had been working in the neighborhood at the time of Marcia's disappearance and had actually been arrested a few weeks later on a separate rape charge that led to a conviction. In addition to the Trimble case, Barrett was also connected to and convicted of the murder of Sarah Des Prez whom he had killed just 3 weeks before Marcia.

The effect that Marcia Trimble's murder had on Nashville still resounds. Metro Nashville Police Captain Mickey Miller perhaps said it best:

"In that moment, Nashville lost its innocence. Our city has never been, and never will be the same again. Every man, woman, and child knew that if something that horrific could happen to that little girl, it could happen to anyone."

MERIWETHER LEWIS MEMORIAL
Milepost 385.9 on Natchez Trace Parkway

This memorial on Meriwether Lewis' grave stands near the approximate site of his controversial death in 1809. As most Americans know, Lewis is one-half of the great pioneer explorer team of Lewis & Clark but the mystery still remains as to what happened the night of October 10th when he stopped at nearby Grinder's Stand on the Natchez Trace after a long day of traveling. Lewis was on his way from the

Louisiana Territory, where he was Governor, toward Washington to settle a few bills that were being questioned by the Department of War. Late that night, Mrs. Grinder, the innkeepers wife (Mr. Grinder was away on business), heard several shots and found Lewis crawling on the floor, begging for water. He had been shot multiple times, once in the head and once in the abdomen and died at sunrise.

While there were no witnesses to anyone else being in the room or on the property other than Lewis' own slaves, conspiracy theorists propose that he was murdered for political reasons. Close friends and associates reported, however, that Lewis had been depressed and had even allegedly attempted suicide numerous times in recent months. Mrs. Grinder even stated that Lewis had acted

strangely throughout the evening, going through spells of agitation and talking to himself. While still unproven after many forensic studies over the centuries, the psychological stress of being revered as a hero on the Corps Of Discovery only to come back and be subjected to a desk job, a mountain of debt, and in some circles, considered a failure for not finding a true Pacific passage may have simply taken it's toll.

Inscription: "Immaturus obi; sed tu felicior annos vive meos: Bona Republica! vive tuos." "I died before my time, but thou

O great and good Republic, live out my years while you live
out your own."

MURDER ON MUSIC ROW

1024 16th Ave S

On March 9, 1989,
Cashbox Magazine
employee Kevin Hughes
was executed in front of
1024 16th Ave, on the
street near what is now
Bobby's Idle Hour after
leaving Evergreen Records
(1021 16th Ave S) with his
friend, Sammy Sadler. Cashbox boss, Richard D'Antonio was
eventually convicted of the crime, which was committed
because Hughes was about to expose D'Antonio's payola
scam.

MUSICA

Buddy Killen Circle at Demonbreun and Division Streets

The earliest purpose of
the area at the
roundabout was as Fort
Houston, an unfinished
Union fortress built upon
the dismantled home of
Russell Houston.
This intersection was
once the hub of all
tourism in Nashville

throughout the 70's and 80's until it fell into disrepair. The
80

Country Music Hall Of Fame moved downtown while BMI built a monolith on its former site. Alan LaQuire was commissioned to create a sculpture for a newly installed roundabout that was to celebrate all genres of music. To the dismay of many, Mr. LaQuire presented "Musica", a 40-foot bronze tangle of 5 clearly male and 4 clearly female nude dancers. Certain organizations are known to dress up the statues in shirts promoting their causes, kilts during St. Patty's Day, etc...

NATHAN BEDFORD FORREST STATUE
East side of I-65 in Brentwood, just south of Harding Road

Considered by many to be the world's ugliest statue, this unsightly fiberglass monument commemorates General Nathaniel Bedford Forrest, the former Confederate general and first national leader of the Ku Klux Klan, riding high on his horse. To top it off, the statue is surrounded by a large display of various Confederate flags. The display stands on a strip of privately held land adjacent to Interstate 65 but can be accessed by an gated road just off of Hogan Road, slightly east of the I-65 overpass, for any brave souls with paint cans and a clean jail record. Since 1995, the statue is constantly getting vandalized and grafitti'd (mostly in February during Black History Month) and has even been shot at several times. The owner of the eyesore is a Nashville attorney who defends his right to have the statue there.

NUN BUN

Bongo Java, 2007 Belmont Boulevard

In 2005, a prankster broke into the Bongo Java Coffee Shop early Christmas morning and made off with the miraculous cinnamon bun in a display case bearing an uncanny resemblance to Mother Teresa. The world-famous "Nun Bun " – as it was relabeled after Mother Teresa objected to commercial promotion of her image - had been on display in the shop since its discovery ten years previous. The bandit has cowardly never been come forward. You won't be in trouble – we just want the Bun back, man.

PATSY CLINE CRASH SITE

Mt. Carmel Road, Camden, TN
I-40 exit 126. Drive north on US Hwy 641 around 15 miles. Cross Hwy 391/1, and you'll see a McDonald's on the right. Just before you reach it, turn left onto Mount Carmel Rd. Drive a little over 2.5 miles. Memorial is on the right.

Right up there with Buddy Holly, Ritchie Valens, and Jim Reeves is the unimaginable plane crash of Country music legend Patsy Cline. She remains one of the most recognizable voices in music history, being one of the first females to have crossover success from Country to Pop. While she lived a life that was subject to rumor and controversy, her death still fascinates fans as she always seemed so untouchable.

On March 5th, 1963, Randy Hughes was piloting the small engine, private plane that held Opry legends Hawkshaw Hawkins, Cowboy Copas, and of course, Mrs. Cline, when they encountered "extremely turbulent weather" around Camden, TN. Witnesses report that they saw the plane circle around with its engine revving and trying to gain altitude before it finally disappeared into the hills. Search parties found the plane early the following morning, which had struck a large tree before digging a 3-foot crater in the earth below. Dean Brewer, the Civil Defense official at the time, was asked about the bodies being located to which he replied, "There's not enough to count...they're all in small pieces." Sections of the plane were found in tree limbs across a 60-yard swath of woods, as were body parts and flesh.

Today, a boulder memorializes the spot where the crash occurred as well as other monuments on the site. For any pop culture junkie, it is definitely worth the hour drive from Nashville to pay tribute to the eternal Queen of Country Music, as well as Hawkins, Copas, and Hughes.

PAUL DENNIS REID

2633 Lebanon Pike (Captain D's)
3470 Lebanon Pike (McDonalds)
2531 Wilma Rudolph Blvd, Clarksville TN (Baskin Robbins)

The most brutal and vicious moments of infamy came by the hands of Nashville's most notorious serial killer, Paul Dennis Reid. Between February and April of 1997, he held the city at a standstill with a series of executions of fast-food employees, the only motive seeming to be petty robbery.

Reid's first attack came on the morning of February 16, 1997 when he came into the Captain D's at 2633 Lebanon Road and told the employees that he was applying for a job. He then forced Sarah Jackson and Steve Hampton into a walk-in cooler, bound their hands, and then shot them execution style before making off with cash from the registers.

Over a month later, Reid approached employees of the 3470 Lebanon Pike location of McDonald's at gunpoint and forced them back into the restaurant, where he bound them as well and shot them in the back of the head. Andrea Brown, Ronald Santiago, and Robert Sewell were among the murdered, while Jose Antonio Ramirez Gonzalez survived when Reid's gun misfired and he was forced to stab Gonzalez, whom he left for dead. A mere $3,000 was taken from the registers.

84

The final attack came another month later in Clarksville, TN at the Baskin Robbins at 2531 Wilma Rudolph Blvd, when Reid kidnapped two employees, Angela Holmes and Michelle Mace, and slit their throats before leaving their bodies in Dunbar Cave State Park.

Reid was captured after an altercation with a former employer, whom Reid attempted to kidnap from his residence. He was charged with 7 counts of murder and is currently awaiting execution at the Morgan County Correctional Complex. His trial was the first to be televised live in the state of Tennessee and his seven death sentences are the most to ever be handed down in the state, as well. It was discovered that Reid was out on parole from the state of Texas and that he had come to Nashville to become, of all things, a Country singer.

PERRY & JANET MARCH HOUSE
3 Blackberry Road

It was from this house that Janet March, the wife of prominent Nashville attorney, Perry March, mysteriously disappeared from on August 15, 1996. Perry claimed that Janet had packed her bags and stormed out of the house, which is why it took him 2 weeks to report the disappearance. However, when Janet's car turned up in a nearby apartment complex and police began to undercover Perry's torrential temper, the suspicion quickly turned toward him. A decade-long pursuit for Janet March's justice wound from Nashville through Chicago and ultimately Ajijic, Mexico, where police arrested Perry March for his wife's

85

murder. His father, Arthur March, was also arrested for helping dispose of the body as well as a conspiracy charge when a plot to kill Janet's parents was also uncovered. Arthur copped a plea deal in exchange for an 18-month sentence, confirming that Perry had killed Janet and that they had disposed of her body in Kentucky. Perry March received a 56-year sentence and will most likely be in his 70's before he is eligible for parole. Janet March's remains have never been found.

PRINTERS ALLEY

The corner of Church St and Printers Alley, between 3rd Ave N and 4th Ave N

In it's earliest days, Printers Alley was exactly that: the hub of Nashville's newspaper, printing and publishing industry. In the late 1800's, it was the dark secret of Nashville's "Men's District"...the part of town that you went to if you were in need of anything, no matter what kind of vice you were trying to appease – alcohol, sex, gambling, murder, political corruption. During prohibition, Printer's Alley was a well-known area to procure the illegal liquor, protected by both police and the mayor.

It wasn't until the 1940's that nightclubs became the more popular spots in the Alley and artists began to use the venues as areas to showcase talent. With clubs like the Black Poodle (once home to the popular burlesque maven, Heaven Lee, and now home to Fiddle & Steel), the Voo Doo Club (now Lonnie's), the Rainbow Room, the Captains Table, the Carousel Club, and the Jolly Roger (now the Dinner Theater), Printers Alley began to set a precedence of quality entertainment in addition to a legacy of debauchery. Back in those days, entertainers such as Chet Atkins, Andy Griffith, and Hank Williams could be heard performing in a number of the clubs. Later on, it was Dottie West, Waylon Jennings, and Barbara Mandrell who all lay claim to being discovered in a bar in Printers Alley, the latter at the Black Poodle (210 Printers Alley) by Billy Sherrill. It is also rumored that the Alley inspired Paul McCartney to write "Sally G" after a tour in the 1970's. More recently, it was in the Bourbon Street Blues Bar that John Rich heard a bartender by the name of Gretchen Wilson belting out some tunes and coerced her to start working with him.

Printer's Alley's most recent low point came in 1998 when David "Skull" Schullman, considered by many to be the "Mayor Of Printer's Alley", was murdered at the Rainbow Room Club (210 Printers Alley) by a two attackers. The assailants were captured but the club never reopened. Reports of a skull-like apparition and Skull's own voice echoing throughout the building have kept tenants away.

In more innocent news, Printers Alley is also home to Nashville's first parking garage as well as the city's first official skyscraper (the Nashville Life & Casualty Building located at 4th and Church).

RICHARD FAGAN & TOM OTERI INCIDENT
204 Burgandy Hill Rd

It was in this house that songwriter, Richard Fagan, known for his hits "Be My Baby Tonight" and "Sold (The Grundy County Auction Incident)" fatally wounded his publisher of 32 years and roommate, Tom Oteri, on April 26, 2008. Both Fagan and Oteri (father of Saturday Night Live cast member, Cheri Oteri) were high on alcohol, as well as prescribed and unprescribed medication, when things became physical between them. Fagan slashed Oteri's wrist in the altercation and, when the bleeding became uncontrollable, drove Oteri to the hospital to be treated. En route, Fagan was arrested for drunk driving and, by the time he was released, Tom Oteri had died.

Richard Fagan was convicted of the drunk driving charge but was appointed to rehab for Oteri's death, after support from Oteri's family convinced the judge that Fagan's addictions were more to blame than Fagan himself. In 2010, Richard Fagan successfully completed rehab, continues to be published by Oteri's son, Tom Oteri Jr., and is a frequent fixture in the Nashville songwriting scene.

ROB BIRONAS CRASH SITE
800 block Battery Lane, on north side of Battery Lane at Dustin Lane intersection.

Another wave of disbelief overcame Nashville when ex-Titans kicker, Rob Bironas, was killed in a single car crash less than a mile from his home on September 20, 2014. The details surrounding the crash were the most distressing, with most locals not wanting to believe the events that were unfolding. At 11:40 pm, country artist Rachel Bradshaw (daughter of NFL great, Terry Bradshaw) called 911 to report that her husband, Bironas, who had said he was going to bed but apparently had left the house around two hours earlier, was missing. Within that time period, 911 had received other calls from multiple motorists, saying a white SUV (assumed to be Bironas' Denali) had nearly run them off the road and was making threatening statements. Moments later, Bironas' vehicle flipped, going westbound on Battery Lane, and came to rest in a ravine across from Dustin Lane at around 11pm. Official reports eventually concluded that the vehicle was travelling at more than 75 mph (where the limit is 35 mph) and that Bironas' alcohol level was at .218%.

Rob Bironas' funeral at Woodlawn was an outpouring of Nashville support and unfortunately, those friends and family have been left with more questions than answers.

SPENCE MANOR
11 Music Sq. E

From the legendary "Elvis Suite" where Elvis spent a number of after-hours adventures during his recording sessions at RCA B around the corner, to studio heads skinny dipping in the guitar-shaped swimming pool, to the filming of

pornography, Spence Manor has seen it all...but its tales are difficult to pull out of anyone who was there. Everyone seems to collectively be a little fuzzy on the details.

What is known of the pool is that Webb Pierce built the guitar-shaped pool here in hopes that it would divert the same tourists who were flocking to his home on Franklin Pike and causing a bit of a nuisance. The attraction failed and was eventually absorbed into the property of Spence Manor.

Now a private condo complex, Spence Manor was once the centerpiece for mischief along Music Row and no doubt has countless mysterious skeletons in its closet. Perhaps one day, in an unauthorized biography or two, the tales will be told.

STEVE MCNAIR MURDERED
105 Lea Avenue, #4

On July 4, 2009, former Tennessee Titans star quarterback, Steve McNair, was murdered at this unit by his mistress, Sahel Kazemi, in a shocking murder/suicide that rattled the Nashville community. Kazemi was a waitress at Dave & Busters in the Opry Mills Mall, where she met McNair and the two of them became involved, unbeknownst to McNair's wife. Kazemi was apparently distraught that McNair was seeing yet *another* woman (other than herself or his wife) and, coupled with financial and debatable other problems, decided the best way to keep him out of the hands of other  women was two shots to his head and 2 to his chest while he was sleeping, before turning the gun on herself.

THE 100 YEAR FLOOD

I-24 Eastbound, just past Blue Hole Road

On May 1st and 2nd, 2010, torrential rains poured down as a severe line of thunderstorms dropped 19 inches of rain over a 48-hour period. As tributaries rose, the Cumberland River itself crested at 51.86 feet, devastating landmarks, historical buildings, and homes across the region. Twenty-one total deaths were reported, while thousands were evacuated, many of them never to return to their homes. The entire downtown area of Nashville was underwater up to 3rd Ave and the Titans stadium across the river was completely flooded, as were the Opryland Hotel and Schermerhorn Symphony Hall. Even millions of dollars in musical instruments belonging to artists such as Keith Urban, Vince Gill, Brad Paisley, Pete Townshend, and Jimi Hendrix stored at the Soundcheck warehouse were ruined beyond repair. In a matter of moments, the 100 Year Flood of Nashville had forever changed the city.

Despite this quickly becoming one of the costliest natural disasters in history, very little media attention was given to flooding due to the BP oil spill that had recently occurred. Nashville's resilience shone through, though, and the city bounced back immediately with an outpouring of local aid and volunteers before the waters began to recede. The residents of the city proved they weren't going to sit around and wait for national aid and executive decisions when they could get it done themselves a whole lot quicker. The resounding cry of

"We are Nashville!" will be a proud motto among residents for years to come.

As news of the flooding finally began to spread around the nation, one of the first jaw-dropping views broadcast on CNN was an entire house floating down a stretch of Interstate 24 (pictured above), just past Blue Hole Road where it crosses what is usually a tiny creek. Many more images and tributes can be found online.

WAYNE MILLS MURDER - PIT & BARREL
515 2nd Ave

The dark side of Nashville's music scene reared its head on November 23, 2013 when local country music favorite, Wayne Mills, was shot in the back of the head at this bar by its owner, Chris Ferrell. Mills was well known in Nashville, having had artists like Jamey Johnson and Blake Shelton open for him on their way up through the ranks. On this particular night, Mills was allegedly intoxicated when an argument ensued concerning Mills smoking in a non-smoking section of the bar. Ferrell claims he fired in self-defense but the autopsy confirmed the shot to the back of the head as well as a significant distance between the gun and the target. Ferrell was arrested and charged with 2nd degree murder; in April of 2015, he was sentenced to 20 years in prison.

Ironically, the Pit & Barrel was just about to be featured on the Spike TV show, Bar Rescue, an episode which showed Ferrell getting upset when being told to remove his guns from the bar. Spike acted properly and never aired the episode.

RANDOM FUN STUFF

"The only time I ever said no was if somebody asked me if I had enough..."
~Sue Brewer

Nothing is more fun than randomness! So here's some random fun stuff...

701 BROOK HOLLOW
www.MusicStartsHere.org

As Nashville tradition would have it, this house at 701 Brook Hollow is a very unassuming spot but contains a tremendous history when you talk to the right people. Since the turn of the 21st century, this house was the location of 112 "3rd Sunday at 3" events, where host (and author of the weekly Nashville blog, MusicStartsHere.com) Doak Turner would invite songwriters, artists, publishers, and industry peeps to hang out, play some songs, and network with each other. In its 9-year run, the house saw a monthly draw of 75 or so songwriters playing songs for 4 hours in 4 rooms, along with their fans and friends, for an estimated total of 8,400 songwriters and over 100,000 songs echoing off its walls over the years.

Some notable alumni of the "3rd Sunday" events: Ira Dean of Trick Pony, Ray Scott, Frankie Ballard, Meghan Linsey of

93

Steel Magnolia, Victoria Shaw, Josh Thompson, Chas Sandford, Jimbeau Hinson, Lance Carpenter, and (ahem) Mason Douglas even attended a time or two. Gary Hannan considered the parties his "good luck charm" since his #1 hits "Tequila Makes Her Clothes Fall Off" and "Back When I Knew It All" were played for the first time at these parties.

But that's not all. A number of hits songs were written there by its tenants: Paul Jefferson wrote the Aaron Tippin hit, "That's As Close As I'll Get To Loving You" at the house, as did house co-owner Steven McClinton with the SIXWIRE hit, "Hey, Look At Me Now". For a time, the Nelson twins (yes,

THOSE Nelson twins) lived the house, as well as Gary Talley of the Box Tops.

And that's *still* not all. The house has also been a recording studio, with countless demos being recorded within its walls, such as the original demo for the Martina McBride hit, "In My Daughter's Eyes" (penned by James Slater) sung as a piano/vocal by Danielle Peck. The Nelson twins recorded their "Life" album here and, in a completely unexpected moment of "Holy crap!", Olivia Newton John recorded a few demos here, as well.

701 Brook Hollow even hosted the aptly named "GuitarBQ's" and "Black Parties" (Halloween extravaganzas) over the years, making it a well-known and well-revered haven for songwriters and the industry.

BELL WITCH CAVE

430 Keysburg Rd, Adams, TN
www.BellWitchCave.com

The "Bell Witch" is the most documented supernatural event in the US and remains one of the most resilient and mysterious legends in Tennessee's history.

The story goes that, in 1804, John Bell moved his family from North Carolina to a farm in Adams, TN near the TN/KY border. Around 1817, the Bell family began to be terrorized by an invisible poltergeist named "Kate" – the Bell Witch. Her hauntings began as simple sounds: chains drug through the house, knocking on the walls, and choking. As news of Kate began to spread throughout the area, neighbors would visit and experience the oddities themselves, often asking questions and receiving answers from Kate herself. It seemed that Kate had come to the Bell's with intent to kill John Bell and to keep Betsy Bell, his youngest daughter, from marrying the wrong boy. Kate did not like Betsy at all and would beat her, pull her hair, and poke her with pins.

When John Bell died of mysterious causes in 1820 – and shortly thereafter, Betsy Bell called off her engagement – the Bell Witch bid farewell and left. She promised to return in 7 years, which she did when she visited John Bell, Jr. for a few weeks in 1828. On this visit, she was very cordial (a "good" witch, if you may), made many premonitions, and even attended church. Upon her departure, she said her return would be in 107 years. However, 1935 rolled around and no run-in with Kate occurred then nor in the years since. If any of this story sounds familiar, it's most likely because the Bell Witch is allegedly the inspiration behind the popular "The Blair Witch Project" and has even inspired two of it's own movies "The Bell Witch Haunting" and "An American Haunting". There have also been countless books researched and written on Kate and her eerie premonitions.

The Bell Witch cave is the last remaining tangible link to Kate. Most scholars familiar with the story believe that she originated from this cave located on the old Bell farm...or at the very least, from the ancient Indian burial ground that is located directly above the cave. A worthwhile tour will tell further details of the legend and take you right into the heart of it, where the Bell children first encountered the witch. For a better thrill, take a nighttime candlelight tour. Just beware when you take photographs in or near the cave as you never know what sights will develop on the picture itself. And make sure you browse the letters hanging in the gift shop from people who have taken stones from the cave...you will surely not want to follow in their footsteps.

BETTY PAGE HIGH SCHOOL

700 Broadway - Hume Fogg

Hume Fogg was not only the first public school in Nashville (as Hume High School), as well as the filming location for Taylor Swift's "Teardrops On My Guitar" video, but it was also the high school that the most famous pin-up girl in history, Ms. Bettie Page, graduated second in her class from in 1940. Bettie (born Betty May Page) grew up in Nashville in a troubled home but was studious and voted "Most Likely To Succeed" by her peers, eventually making her way through Peabody College (now part of Vanderbilt), and onto worldwide stardom and garage calendars everywhere.

Other famous alumni include Pat Boone, Dinah Shore, and Phil Harris.

MUSIC ROW: THE BOAR'S NEST
911b 18th Ave S.

According to her biography at the Nashville Songwriters Hall Of Fame, *"Sue Brewer was a champion of many songwriters in Nashville. She opened her heart, home, and pocket book to many a struggling country western artists. Brewer managed George Jones's club, Possum Holler, worked at the "Music City News" trade paper, and made her home, which she dubbed the "Boar's Nest," an open house for songwriters. Sue hosted guitar pulls in her living room where writers like Waylon Jennings, Kris Kristofferson, Faron Young, George Jones, Roger Miller, Merle Kilgore, and Jack Clemente gathered together to try out their latest songs."* And according to Waylon's biography, Sue was also set on revenge against an ex-boyfriend, to whom she swore after the breakup that she'd sleep with every Opry star in town. Upstairs at this now vacant location was the Boar's Nest, which had Sue's infamous conquests in 8x10's hanging on the living room wall: her "Wall of Fame".

BOULDER TOMBSTONE

1001 4th Ave. S.

Drive straight in for three blocks, and look for the rock topped by a small metal lantern.

This out-of-place boulder sits in the Nashville City Cemetery at the memorial of Ann Rawlins Sanders 1815-1836...or so says it's engraving. According to legend, Ann committed suicide by jumping off of a cliff after a quarrel with her

fiancé, Charles H. Sanders. In memoriam, Charles brought the rock she jumped off of to her grave and placed a lantern atop it as Ann was afraid of the dark. That alone makes for an interesting landmark. However, the mystery deepens...

A cemetery keeper in the early 1900's claimed that the plot belongs to Edward Steele and that his wife, Marion Steele, is the one buried under the boulder; Ann Rawlins is actually buried in a plot nearby. As to why Ann's name is carved in the boulder on top of Marion's grave has been lost in history.

BOURBON STREET BLUES AND BOOGIE BAR

220 Printers Alley

John Rich saw Gretchen Wilson for the first time when she hopped on stage one night and blew the roof of this iconic

98

Nashville blues club. He heavily pursued her for weeks until she finally caved in and started working with him.

BUDWEISER FROGS
7 Music Sq. W

Tom Woodard: "The phone rang, it was a call from Michael Smith and Dave Swain with DMB&B from Saint Louis. We had done a ton of music tracks for their clients up until that day. They were good friends. They asked if I could make a frog say Budweiser and we discussed three sitting on a lily pad... I lived on a farm with a small pond on it here in Tennessee filled with frogs. I knew exactly what the spot was supposed to sound like. Lay down a bed of crickets, splatter some ambient sounds of frogs bellowing in the background, and then have the three syllables uttered in the right sequence...

Thanks Michael and Dave for my fifteen minutes of fame. It's been a cool to have a great story to have around the rest of my life. "You're really the voice of 'Bud'?!", I get asked when it comes up with my friends and family. It's awesome. America, what a country...

Ronnie Brooks ("weis") and Brian Steckler, ("er"), were added to the voices, which were recorded in a studio that was at 7 Music Sq. W. The audio was complete. Michael Smith took that track and three pencil drawings of frogs into the Anheuser Busch offices in the next few days and the spot was born. Three Nashville voices were changed, forever.

The spot was never meant to be a campaign...it was just supposed to be a spot, not even a Super Bowl spot at that. Then the agency hired Stan Winston, the creator of animatronics (Jurassic Park and Congo)...remember, this was

1995, when that technology was just beginning. He created the frogs themselves.

For seven years, the campaign grew and changed agency hands from DMB&B to DDB Needham/Chicago to Goodby Silverstein to a tragic end in the swamp at the hand of those lizards. It was a great run and a true blessing. I got to work with guys like Stan Winston and Gore Verbinski on spots and the two incredibly creative and full of life guys, Michael Smith and Dave Swain...thanks again guys.   ~"BUD"

*Author's note: the house at this address was demolished in late 2015 to make way for a new hotel.

CASTLE GWYNN

2124 New Castle Road, Arrington, TN
www.TNRenFest.com

Once of the most unexpected sights in Middle Tennessee unfolds on I-840 between Murfreesboro and Triune. As you travel westward, surely your eyes will mistake you – for those blinding white bricks, towering spires, and unmistakable turrets can't surely be...why, yes it is...a castle!

What you are seeing is "Castle Gwynn", a replica of a 12th century Welsh border castle, and is the result of over 40 years of dreaming and doing by it's owner resident, Michael Freeman. Michael first imagined the castle in a sketch for his high school architecture class in 1970 but didn't begin work on the actual structure itself in 1980. He and his wife, Jackie, have been slowly building...then working more and saving...then building and spending...then working and saving...to build this epic edifice slowly but surely for over 33 years.

Highlights of the castle include handmade floor tiles, brick arches (including 14,000 bricks hand-molded and laid into 60 arches in the kitchen alone), a collection of 16th century swords, tapestries, artwork, and stained glass windows.

As this is Mr. and Mrs. Freeman's personal residence, daily tours are not permitted. However, if you're around in May, you're in luck! Every year, the castle hosts the Tennessee Renaissance Festival where not only can you experience jousting, games, artisans, and flavors of the olden days but you can also tour Castle Gwynn. Visit TNRenFest.com for more info.

Photo Credit: Michael Freeman

MUSIC ROW: CHET ATKINS OFFICE
1013 17th Ave S.

The office of Chet Atkins for a number of years.

COURTYARD CAFE
867 Bell Rd

Before they gave us Dierks' "Feel That Fire", McGraw's "Felt Good On My Lips", and Toby's "Red Solo Cup", the Warren Brothers cut their chops at this awesome Italian eatery back in the late 90's before landing a recording deal with BNA Records. Unfortunately, that semi-legendary status alone couldn't keep the restaurant open and the building was

eventually razed. The site is just behind the Zaxby's that is at the location.

DAVE RAMSEY HEADQUARTERS
1749 Mallory Lane, Franklin TN

The #1 financial radio talk show in the US, the Dave Ramsey Show, is based out of this building, with Dave himself welcoming listeners and visitors into Financial Peace Plaza to watch him broadcast his worldwide syndicated program. Dave has been on the air since 1992, developing his loyal listenership from flagship station, WTN, until 2013 when he set off on his own, becoming one of the biggest shows to self-syndicate without the support of a national network.

Visitors to Financial Peace Plaza can schedule their moment to scream "We're debt free!!" on the air, visit a bookstore that

carries all of the Dave Ramsey products, and enjoy free coffee and baked goods at Martha's Place.

DEMONBREUN'S CAVE
1707 River Hills Dr
Across the street and down on the riverbank.

The first residence of Timothy Demonbreun, (Nashville's first white resident) in Nashville was technically this cave, which is still visible on the banks of the Cumberland River. The verdict is still out as to if Demonbreun, his family, and all his crew made permanent use of the cave but it is known that he evaded Indian attacks for weeks at a time inside of it.

While accessible only via the river itself (think kayak or canoe, if visiting), you can get pretty close by following a flight of concrete stairs down to an old river landing off of River Hills Dr. Be careful as the rocks are pretty treacherous off the landing. There is also a good view from the

far side of the river, near where the Shelby Bottoms Greenway and the natural trail split.

Inscription: Jaques-Timothe De Montbrun, French Canadian fur trader and later lieutenant governor of the Illinois Country, visited in this area as early as 1769. On at least one occasion he took refuge in the cave 0.9 mile N. when attacked by Indians. He settled in Nashville in 1790, living there until his death in 1826.

EL CHICO
1132 Old Murfreesboro Rd

It's not uncommon to seeing a rising star performing on the patio of this local location of the El Chico franchise. Chris Young had a standing gig here when he went to MTSU, with  Lee Brice being a frequent performer, as well as Buddy Jewell. This might be one Mexican place where you *do* want to drink the water.

ERNEST P. WORRELL
1219 & 1220 McGavock St
www.HeyVernItsErnest.com

Alright, pay attention – this one's a good one. In 1980, on the 2nd floor of this brownstone building at the corner of McGavock and 13th, John Cherry of the advertising agency, Carden & Cherry, was tasked with devising a campaign to steer thrill-seekers to a struggling theme park in Kentucky named Beech Bend Park. His answer came in the form of an unforgettably lovable yet absent-minded redneck named Ernest P. Worrell. Although the theme park campaign didn't quite hit home, Purity Dairies (360 Murfreesboro Rd) took the reins with Ernest and made him along with his portrayer, Jim Varney, a household name by using them in their regional dairy campaigns.

Most of the early commercials were initially shot at a house off of Hazelwood Circle near Franklin Road. National campaigns such as Mello Yello and Sprite soon followed – another house off of Davidson Road in West Nashville became the primary location for hundreds of commercials as Cherry, his business partner, Jerry Carden, Varney, Ernest, and the unseen neighbor, Vern, promoted products.

A Saturday morning kids show called *Hey Vern, It's Ernest!* was soon produced and filmed in a prefab (and long gone) studio near the Tennessee State Fairgrounds. Feature film movie scripts were written as local locations became backdrops for films such as *Ernest Goes To Jail*, *Ernest Goes To Camp*, and *Ernest Scared Stupid* (see MUSIC CITY MOVIES section). This even put the Ernest legacy in the Guinness Book of World Records as the "First Film Based On An Advertisement". Ernest became the well-intended heart, the love, and laughter inside all of us as well as a face of resilience when things don't quite go as planned.

For an in-depth recollection of the "Ernest" experience, as well as hilarious memoirs with the unparalleled talent of the great Jim Varney, make sure you check out John Cherry's book, *Keeper Of The Clown*.

FIRST CRACKER BARREL

401 Hwy 109, Lebanon TN (first location, now a Citgo)
305 Hartman Dr, Lebanon TN (Headquarters)

The worldwide headquarters of the home-cooking roadtrip restaurant of choice, Cracker Barrel, is located in nearby Lebanon, TN, close to its first location near I-40. In 1969, Dan Evins opened the first Cracker Barrel store as a place where travelers could get trusted goods and foods on their way across the new interstate system. Part country store, part trading post, Dan ensured his restaurant would reflect the American heritage and offer quality recipes like scratch biscuits & gravy, chicken-fried everything, and this author's favorite, the Sunrise Sampler. Today, there are over 600 stores in 42 states, all preserving a little slice of Americana (and pie!) in each one.

One fascinating purpose of the 90-acre headquarters is to not only display the original Cracker Barrel sign but also to warehouse the thousands of "picker" antique items that get sorted, cleaned, and shipped to decorate the stores, both old and new.

GIGI'S CUPCAKES
1816 Broadway
www.GigisCupcakesUSA.com

Gina "Gigi" Butler original came to Nashville to become the next country music star (who doesn't?) and ended up with one of the most popular cupcake companies in America, with 98 nationwide locations and counting. Gigi moved to

Nashville from California in 1994 and, after a decade of singing honky tonks, cleaning houses, and working at Red Lobster, she finally set her mind on the cupcake business. Following family recipes from great, great aunts all the way to experimenting recipes with her mother (which she continues to do), Gigi opened the original location for Gigi's Cupcakes at this store in Midtown on February 21, 2008, with $33 left in her pocket and some tightly crossed fingers. 98 locations later and $43 million in sales in 2013, you can often find Gigi herself still baking cupcakes and serving customers behind this counter.

GUITARTOWN PROJECT
All around town

As you explore Nashville, you're bound to notice the vast number of large, oversize guitars marking street corners and sidewalks. These 10-foot high fiberglass decorative Gibson (Les Paul or Chet Atkins model) guitars were individually designed by local and national artists to benefit the GuitarTown Project back in 2004. Initially, they were placed in front of city landmarks, each having a certain theme or musical artist, such as George Jones, Johnny Cash, Dolly Parton, and Elvis associated with the chosen design.

In 2006, Gibson auctioned off the guitars and raised over $400,000 for the Country Music Hall of Fame, the DISTRICT, the Cystic Fibrosis Foundation, and the United Way of Nashville.

In 2007, someone managed to cut the protective lock, break the guitar from the concrete foundation, and steal the LeAnn Rimes-themed guitar from in front of Curb Records. As of this printing, the guitar has not been returned.

The current lineup of guitars and locations can be found on Gibson.com.

JIMMY HOFFA'S TRIAL LOCATION

801 Broadway
US District Court

The biggest trial in Nashville history took place here when Teamsters President Jimmy Hoffa and Robert Kennedy came to town in October of 1962. Kennedy, Attorney General and chief counsel to the McClelland Committee investigating labor corruption, had Hoffa being tried for the 4th time, already having failed previously on numerous counts of bribery and wiretapping. This time, Hoffa had been accused of setting up a dummy

corporation in Nashville (Test Fleet Corporation) to launder a bribe from Commercial Carriers that was paid to Hoffa to settle a strike.

The trial had its share of drama: a failed assassination attempt on Hoffa by a mentally-unstable Warren Swanson...no less than two jurors dismissed on suspicion that Hoffa had tried to rig the jury (it was later alleged that Hoffa's local rising-star attorney, Tommy Osborn, was involved as well)...and ultimately, a mistrial called from a hung-jury. Hoffa was finally convicted at his retrial in Chattanooga but the circus he created in Nashville still carries the twists, turns, and deceptions of any good made-for-TV law thriller.

Of note, during his trial, Hoffa stayed on the 7th floor of the Jackson Hotel (SE corner of 6th and Deadrick).

MELROSE SPRING
Woodlawn Cemetery
660 Thompson Lane
Enter the Woodlawn Cemetery on the North side of Thompson Lane. Stay on the main drive and go past the funeral home. Turn left at the four-way stop after the funeral home and homestead is about 100 yards up on the left.

A surprising little jewel of Nashville history lies in the middle of Woodlawn Cemetery, tucked away in a small oasis merely feet from the final resting places of Marty Robbins, Dobie Gray, and Porter Waggoner. An original springhouse sits over a bubbling spring that was used as a hospital site during the Civil War. The property was once occupied by Tennessee Governor Aaron Brown in the 1840's long before being bought and restored by Lillian and George Forehand in the 1960's. The Forehand's moved a few historic cabins (and a working mill) to the site, had the plaques inscribed, and built the adjacent pond, complete with ducks. The cemetery did not grow around the site until years later but the combination makes this springhouse a truly remarkable hidden treasure in a completely unexpected place.

Inscription: "Melrose. Former Home of Gov. Aaron V. Brown. The Confederate Works ran 200 yards south of the residence. Thence turned west so as to pass in front of Berry Home."

Inscription #2: "HOSPITAL WATER SOURCE. Because of the Generous Water Supply available from this spring, the area around it was selected as a hospital site for treatment of soldiers wounded in the Battle of Nashville which took place during the War Between the States."

MELROSE SPRING: CARPER HOMESTEAD
Woodlawn Cemetery
660 Thompson Lane

Inscription: Known to be one of the oldest houses remaining from the early American Era, originally located on Cane Ridge Road at Antioch, Tennessee. The Materials were removed piece-by-piece and rebuilt exactly as it stood when occupied by the Carper Generations. Donated to Woodlawn Memorial Park for Historic Preservation by the children of William Washington and Susie Black Carper. Dedicated 1969.

MOONLANDING SOCKS
427 Chestnut St

In the heart of the re-blooming Wedgewood-Houston neighborhood, the 100-year old building on this site used to house the Nashville  location of the May Hosiery Mill, a factory that most notably...wait for it...wove the socks for the astronauts that landed on the moon in 1969. The mill closed in 1980 and is now casually known as "Chestnut Square", housing art galleries and artist studios.

THE MOORE MAN
2nd Ave N and Broadway

This is a local landmark and a remnant of the Phillips and Quarles Hardware Company who occupied the building previous to the current tenant, the Hard Rock Café. The Hard Rock Café gift shop building is a segment leftover from George Dickel's (yes, THAT George Dickel) original "Silver Dollar Saloon" built in 1890, popularized by silver dollars in every other floor tile.

MUSIC CITY WALK OF FAME PARK

4th Ave S, just north of the Country Music Hall Of Fame

This park and honor is Nashville's version of the "Hollywood star" for contributions to the cities music industry and heritage. Established in November of 2006, the first class of inductees included Reba McEntire, Ronnie Milsap, and Roy Orbison, amongst others and has grown by 10 to 12 new additions every year.
Ceremonies happen twice a year and visitors can be notified of as well as nominate new honorees via the VisitMusicCity.com website.

NASHVILLE PALACE

2400 Music Valley Dr (original location)
2611 McGavock Pike (new location)
www.NashvillePalace.net

Before the Nashville Palace occupied its current location on McGavock Pike, it was in its original location where the Caney Fork Restaurant is now. Opened in 1977, it was here that up-and-coming artists like Garth Brooks, Brad Paisley, Sawyer Brown, Ricky Van Shelton, and Patty Loveless would perform and more tenured artists such as Johnny Cash,

Jimmy Dean, Eddy Arnold, Jimmy Dickens, Tammy Wynette, Willie Nelson, Ernest Tubb, and many, many others would just hang out. Jerry Reed played the Palace 30 times the year it opened and a 17-year-old Lorrie Morgan got the "first time jitters" at the Palace. Webb Pierce was such a

regular that he had his own cooler in the back of the bar. A pre-superstar Alan Jackson even slept in his van in the parking lot, waiting for an opportunity to play on the stage here; he has often quoted the Nashville Palace as the place where he got his start.

One of the most legendary stories in Nashville lore is that of Randy Traywick, a dishwasher at the old Palace that would

hop onstage during his shift to sing a song or two. Traywick even managed to record a live album here called "Live At The Nashville Palace", which his manager/wife, Liv Hatcher (who also worked at the Palace at the time) used to get Randy a record deal with Warner Bros. The record label preferred he use a new name, though: Randy Travis.

NATCHEZ TRACE PARKWAY BRIDGE

.7 miles from the northern terminus of the Natchez Trace Parkway

This bridge, also known as the Natchez Trace Parkway Arches, is one of the most spectacular visual sites in the Middle Tennessee area. Located on the beautiful Natchez

Trace Parkway, it channels drivers and bikers 155 feet over Highway 96 across what its industry deemed the "single most outstanding achievement in the bridge industry in 1994". It is the first segmentally constructed concrete arch bridge in the US, made up of 122 hollow segments weighing up to 41 tons each.

There is a pull-off on the north side of the Trace to view the bridge but the most awe-inspiring way to see it is to travel Highway 96 and go under it.

OPRYLAND PARK REMNANTS

Parking lot walkway between Opry Mills Mall and the Gaylord Opryland Resort

One of the great draws to Nashville was the Opryland Theme Park, a giant entertainment complex built primarily out of necessity for a new home for the Grand Ole Opry. Opened in 1972, the park had an impressive share of roller coasters, water rides, and bumper cars. Naturally, many country music stars, like Diamond Rio and Little Texas, got their starts as performers at the Opryland Theme Park. Even though attendance to the park grew to draw 2 millions visitors annually, competition from other regional amusement parks (like Dolly Parton's *Dollywood*), the lack of any expansion room, and the  seasonality of it led to it's closure on December 31, 1997. The park was demolished and the year-round Opry Mills Mall was put in it's place, with the mall mainly where the park's parking lot used to be and the mall's parking lot where the rides used to be.

Up until November of 2011, there were still a few remnants that could be seen. Most notably, the canyon of the Grizzly River Rampage (which was host to a qualifying event for the whitewater event of the 1996 Olympics) was clearly visible along the connecting path between the mall and the resort but was removed after a new building was built over them. Other structures such as the historic Gaslight and Roy Acuff Theaters stood for 14 years after the removal of the park until the 2010 flood destroyed them. Today, the only remaining visible structures left from the original park are the concrete levee tracing along the mall grounds and the railroad embankment that can be seen when entering the complex from the McGavock entrance.

PIANO STAIRS

322 Broadway – Jimmy Buffett's Margaritaville Nashville

If you don't know they're there, you might think you're imagining things...are those musical notes matching your steps as you ascend the alternating black and white stairs up to the second floor of this downtown establishment?! Couldn't be. However, if you're a believer, you can make your own music with some quick steps and a melody in your head. Grab a partner and attempt some Beethoven! Or just give the ol' chromatic scale a shot. Regardless of your ability to tickle the ivories with your twinkle toes, these are just a fun one to try out.

MUSIC ROW: RANDY TRAVIS HOUSE

1610 16th Ave. S

Randy Travis and his future wife, Liv, lived here prior to him signing with Warner Bros.

RED DOOR SALOON

1816 Division St.

Not only is the Red Door Saloon a great place to hang out
and have a beer or three, but it holds a horrifying secret
beneath its floors. Brave visitors can experience this secret
by finding the peephole in the middle of the floor and
peering into the dark. The deal is that no one can tell you
what is there...and if you are courageous enough to see it for
yourself, you canNOT tell anyone else what you saw. You
have to kneel down in front of everyone in the middle of the
bar and see it for yourself! All I can tell you is: one is real,
the other is not.

SHONEYS

1521 Demonbreun St.

Back in the glory days of Nashville, a fresh-off-the-bus,
wannabe Country star would roll into town and their first
stop would no doubt be the Shoney's restaurant that used to
sit in this parking lot. It was the go-to gathering place just
off Music Row where the casual clientele ranged from Harlan
Howard to Bon Jovi. Adjacent to the restaurant was the

Shoney's Inn (now a
Comfort Inn), where
the same young
wannabe's would stay
their first few weeks
in Nashville. While
the restaurant never
quite reached
"Historical Landmark"
status (it was
demolished in 2003), it's immortalized in pop culture,
captured in thousands of photographs of the old

Demonbreun St, in Joe Diffie's song "Third Rock From The Sun", and as the site where Tracy Lawrence was shot in an alleged robbery attempt.

SMALL WORLD HOUSE
1644 Chickering Road

One of the most unusual designs of modern architecture in Nashville is this house near Warner Park, informally designated the "Small World house". While it's neighbors are far more modern and conservative, the Small World house is fashioned from odd shapes, forms, cones, shrubs, and bubble windows similar to the popular ride at Disneyland, "It's A Small World". "Why?", one might ask? First, the house was built by Richard and Rhonda Small (get it?!). And second, sometimes the better question is: "Why not!".

SNOWBALL THROWING BEARS
Edgehill and 12 Ave. S
1229 6th Ave N.

Guarding the entrance to a retirement home, these very random bears are frozen in the middle of a vicious snowball fight. During holidays, you may even find them clothed in appropriate attire to match the season. They were originally a set of 4 that decorated the Polar Bear Frozen Custard Shops in 1930 but were relocated multiple times throughout the years with these two landing here and a third being perched in Germantown at 1229 6th Ave N. The location of the original 4th bear remains a mystery.

THIRD MAN RECORDS

623 7th Ave S
www.ThirdManRecords.com

Alt-Rock icon, Jack White, opened his combination record label/music store/performance venue, Third Man Records, here in 2009. Specializing in vinyl releases of its artists, Third Man is home to artists Karen Elson, The Raconteurs, and Conan O'Brien (yes, that Conan) and also features select "Blue-Series" artists who can record a track or two as they pass through Nashville and have it produced and released by White on the TMR label. A visitor to the store will encounter a plethora of vinyl options, the Novelties lounge (featuring a

vintage Scopitone machine as well as a DIY phonograph booth), and sometimes even Mr. White himself.

TIN ROOF PLAQUE
1516 Demonbreun St – 4th booth on the right in main door

Pop into Tin Roof on Demonbreun and make sure you get a pic of the plaque that's on the 4th booth on the right. "Back in the day", as they like to call it, a group of buds that consisted of the folks commemorated on the plaque, used to sit at that very table and are assumed to have had a lot of drinks. Guys like Lee Brice and Kyle Jacobs, as well as Detox from Halfway To Hazard – and girls like Vicky McGehee – were in this group and used this very table as home base during their "up and coming" years. Maybe there's still a little mojo hanging around the booth for all the future up-and-comers.

TRIGGER
49 Music Sq. W

Roy Rogers' famous horse, Trigger, was long on display as the main draw at the Roy Rogers/Dale Evans Music in Victorville, CA and later, Branson, MO. Trigger was featured in

every Roy Rogers film, ridden by Rogers himself, finding his own diehard fan base amongst cowboys and cowgirls. Upon

119

his death, Trigger's hide was stretched over a plaster cast and put on display, along with Buttermilk (Dale's horse) and Bullet (their dog), drawing 200,000 visitors a year to the museum. When the museum went out of business in 2010, Trigger was auctioned for $266,500 to RFD-TV (along with Buttermilk and Bullet), who puts the animals on display at remote events, as well as an occasional appearance at their headquarters in Nashville.

UNITED RECORD PRESSING
453 Chestnut St
www.URPressing.com

The United Record Pressing plant is one of the "Must See" tours that a Nashville visitor (and resident!) should run to.

Opened in 1949, URP pressed the first 7" Beatles records in 1962 and went on to be the site where artists like Hank Williams, Jr. and Wayne Newton signed their record deals in the resident "Party Room". One of the most fascinating attractions in the building is the "Motown Suite" where Marvin Gaye, the Supremes, the Four Tops, Stevie Wonder, and Smokey Robinson all stayed due to the south having limited accommodations for African-American artists in the '60s. A large amount of the furniture and antique equipment is original...as are the mysterious shoes found in the Motown apartment bedroom.

Tours of United Record Pressing are available for $5 per person on Tuesdays at 2PM and at 11AM on Fridays. Other times can be scheduled for large groups by emailing united@urpressing.com or calling 866-407-3165.

US NAVAL RESERVE TRAINING CENTER
Shelby Park

It's not everyday that one can see a Naval ship on a random street in Middle Tennessee. Luckily, the Navy helped Nashville out and built this training center in 1948. According to its registration for the National Register of Historic Places, "The south façade is the most distinctive of the building, featuring forty-four bays and a large projection at the center designed to resemble the prow of a ship. The 'bow' of the building, which looks onto the Cumberland River, is built to resemble the nose of a heavy warship, ploughing through the waters —complete even to a captain's bridge above prow, with a signal-hoist and yardarm. A railing that furthers the appearance of a ship is present around the deck. The windows of the ship's prow are replacements that date to c. 1982, but are set within original openings and resemble the bands of metal-and-glass windows of the original structure. The tip of the prow nearly reaches Davidson Road, and is only separated by a chain link and barbed wire fence."

WHITE BRIDGE

From Hwy 70, take White Bridge Pike west – bridge will be immediately on right as part of the Richland Creek Greenway.

Staying true to the "random" theme of this section, the actual white bridge of "White Bridge Road" fame is located at the trailhead of the Richland Creek Greenway, ¼ mile away from the Dutchman's Curve train wreck site. When it was built in 1913 by Howard Jones (who also built the Shelby Street Bridge), it was a vital link for West Nashville transit across Richland Creek and the railroad. Cars are not allowed

to drive over it anymore but it is still accessible as a pedestrian bridge crossing the same creek and tracks it has for a century. And it is still white, of course.

WILLIE NELSON FORTUNE TELLER

325 Broadway
inside Dixieland Delights

Want Willie Nelson to tell you your fortune? Just head on down to Broadway and pop inside the Dixieland Delights store! Willie's in the back, waiting to solve your mystery. A mere $1 per fortune is a small price to pay for something none of your friends have ever done.

CELEBRITY HOUSES

These are houses that are either lived in or were once lived in by the respective Nashvillian. Some of these properties are easily visible from public roads so explore and view at your own risk. However, many of them are very private so please do NOT trespass. And if you do, don't leave a copy of this guidebook behind.

Roy Acuff
3940 Moss Rose Dr

Jason Aldean
4637 Reed Rd,
Thompson's Station

Gary Allan
114 Walnut Dr, Hendersonville

Dierks Bentley
4410 Granny White Pike
4225 Franklin Pike (future)

Congresswoman Diane Black
1254 Wavecrest Cir, Gallatin

Clint Black/Lisa Hartman Black
141 Chickering Meadows

Garth Brooks
1250 Genelle Dr
Goodlettsville

Glen Campbell
827 Battery Lane

Johnny Cash
200 Caudill Dr
Hendersonville

Kenny Chesney
400 Lake Valley Dr, Franklin
9635 Stanfield Rd

Kelly Clarkson
123 Summit Ln, Hendersonville,

Patsy Cline
815 Nella Drive

Lorianne Crook
1111 Wilson Pike

Sheryl Crow
6662 Cross Keys Rd, College Grove

Billy Ray & Miley Cyrus
1749 Thompson Station Rd W, Thompson Station

Charlie Daniels
16832 Central Pike, Mt Juliet

Johnny Depp
2467 Hidden River Lane, Franklin

Little Jimmy Dickens
5010 W Concord Rd

Ronnie Dunn
2281 Old Hickory Blvd
5103 Heathrow Blvd (former)

Sara Evans
1021 White Hall Dr, Franklin (prev)

Ben Folds
2700 Westwood Ave (prev)

Jared Followill
3540 Trimble Rd

Matthew Followill
874 S Curtiswood Lane

Peter Frampton
9184 Brushboro Ct

Senator Bill Frist
703 Bowling

Simon Fuller
The Adelicia, 900 20th Ave S. #1705

Vince Gill/Amy Grant
515 Park Center Dr

Al Gore
312 Lynnwood Blvd

Governor's Mansion
882 Curtiswood Lane

Emmylou Harris
1709 Graybar Ln

Julianne Hough
The Adelicia, 900 20th Ave S.

Alan Jackson
1256 Moran Rd, Franklin

Stonewall Jackson
6007 Cloverland Dr

Waylon Jennings/Jesse Colter
824 West Hillview Dr

George Jones
4025 Nestledowns Dr, Franklin
4121 Franklin Pike – (former, with Tammy Wynette)
5097 Heathrow (former)

The Judds
5750 (Ashley)/5728 (Naomi) Garrison Rd,
5601 Pinewood Rd (Wynonna), Leipers Fork

Charles Kelley
4415 Tyne Blvd

Ke$ha
933 Forest Acres Court
5739 Cloverhill Dr (childhood)

Kid Rock
105 West End Circle

Miranda Lambert
23 Governor's Way (gated)

Brenda Lee
306, 308, & 314 Elberta St

Little Richard
121 4th Ave S. Occasionally lives in the penthouse of the
Downtown Hilton.

Barbara Mandrell
2 Goldstone Court
Fontanel (FontanelMansion.com) – 4225 Whites Creek Pike
(prev)

Martina McBride
4409 Franklin Pike

Delbert McClinton
1101 Ridgeview Dr

Michael McDonald
3309 Boyd Mill Pike, Franklin

Reba McEntire
175 Cherokee Dock Rd, Gallatin

Ronnie Milsap
806 N. Curtiswood Lane

Tim McGraw/Faith Hill
4009 Carters Creek Pike, Franklin (prev)
4406 Chickering Lane
1152 Crater Hill Dr.

Paul Overstreet
1485 Cedar Hill Rd, Kingston Springs

Brad Paisley
Approx 120 Glen Haven Dr

Dolly Parton
9510 Crockett Rd

Minnie Pearl
874 S. Curtiswood Lane

Luke Perry
3830 Sylvia Rd, Dickson

Kellie Pickler
4102 Sneed Rd.

130

Curly Putman
4391 Franklin Rd, Lebanon

Dave Ramsey
513 King Richards Ct

John Rich
3432 Love Cir

LeAnn Rimes
512 King Richards Ct (prev)

Tex Ritter
899 Curtiswood Lane

Thomas Ryman
NE Corner of 2nd Ave S & Lea Ave

Hillary Scott
1008 Liberty Church Trail

Blake Shelton
23 Governor's Way (gated)

Donna Summer
9814 Split Log Rd, Brentwood, TN

Taylor Swift
1 Northumberland (gated)
The Adelicia, 900 20th Ave S #1710
173 Inlet Dr, Hendersonville (prev)
211 Bowling (bought for mom)

Carrie Underwood
8 Wentworth Pl (gated)
608 Clareese Park Pl, Franklin (prev)
New property: Pinewood Rd, approx 1 mile west of Natchez
Trace intersection

Keith Urban/Nicole Kidman
27 Northumberland

Steven Tyler
4501 Beacon

Jim Varney
501 Hickory Springs Rd, White House

Darrell Waltrip
110 Deerfield Ct, Franklin

Jack White
5055 Franklin Pike

Hank Williams Sr
4916 Franklin Pike

Hayley Williams
926 Fair St, Franklin

Oprah Winfrey
1413 Willowbrooke Cir, Franklin

Steve Winwood
1865 Laurel Ridge Dr,

132

Reese Witherspoon
3625 Woodmont Blvd (childhood home)
851 Curtiswood Ln (current)

Tammy Wynette
4916 Franklin Pike

Trisha Yearwood
9324 Concord Rd

FILM & TV

Nashville has true potential to be a film location Mecca if state legislation would ever be passed to allow the needed tax incentives to attract filmmakers. Despite the ball-dropping, some very recognizable and even blockbuster hits (and television shows) have been filmed in or around Nashville. The now-defunct Tennessee State Prison hosts the majority of these films but, hey, we'll take what we can get.

Photo Credit: Sean L. Smith Photography

COAL MINER'S DAUGHTER

Sissy Spacek makes an unforgettable performance as Loretta Lynn in the latter's life-story, *Coal Miner's Daughter*. Nashville also makes a number of on-location impressions, starting off with cameos in the Ryman Auditorium, scenes with the great Merle Kilgore inside Tootsie's Orchid Lounge, and an appearance by Ernest Tubb himself on the back stage at Ernest Tubb's Record Shop across Broadway. There is also a honeymoon scene at a motor lodge that used to sit in Cool Springs just north of the corner of Moore's Lane and Franklin Road, now a garden store.

ERNEST GOES TO CAMP

Filmed at the campgrounds of Montgomery Bell State Park and Camp Marymount in Fairview, TN.

ERNEST GOES TO JAIL

The bank featured in the movie is now a Bank of America located 4405 Memphis-Bristol Hwy with interiors done in a warehouse off of Elliston Parkway. Ernest's house is located at 805 N. 6th St and is easily recognizable. The exterior of the prison is an obvious location: the Tennessee State Prison served for the yard scenes, although the interior "cell block" scenes were filmed in the top floor of the Metro Courthouse downtown.

136

East Nashville was primarily featured as the town of "Briarville" where Ernest saves the day by destroying monsters with milk. Shelby Park served as the outdoor woods scenes while the same warehouse off of Ellington Parkway that was used for the bank interior of the jail in "Ernest Goes To Jail" was home to the interiors.

Briarville Town Square is the main drag of 5 Points, with the Briarville Sheriff Department at 1017 Woodland St (currently Margot Café). The scene where Ernest lets his mopping invention get the best of him was filmed in the parking lot of what is now Beyond The Edge at 112 S. 11th St.

Old Lady Hackmore's house, once a burned out pillared shell as it was for filming, is an unmistakable remodeled beauty located on the east side of Franklin Pike, about a half mile north of Harding Pike.

The carport where Kenny gets attacked by the troll in the boat is located at 6525 Jocelyn Hollow Rd (although establishing shots were of the house next door).
The grocery store used for filming is now Bill Martin's Corner Store at 1105 Fatherland Dr.
Briarville Elementary school is actually Robertson Academy, chosen due to writer/director John R. Cherry III's and Daniel Butler's (who played the Sheriff in the film) sons having both attended the Academy.

You can also catch a quick glimpse of Hillsboro Village back in the old day when Ernest drives his truck through the intersection of 21st & Acklen in a frantic scene.

THE GREEN MILE

The Tennessee State Prison makes yet another recognizable film appearance in this Oscar-nominated masterpiece starring Tom Hanks and Michael Clarke Duncan.

Gary Sinese's house is located on 2463 Liberty Valley Road near Lewisburg, TN.

The cemetery is Round Hill Cemetery in Belfast, TN.

Other houses used are located in Nolensville, TN and Shelbyville, TN.

NOT IN NASHVILLE: The nursing home is really the Flat Top Manor in Blowing Rock, NC.

HANNAH MONTANA – THE MOVIE

Smiley Hollow – 5937 Smiley Hollow Rd, Goodlettsville

According to production notes: *"Another key location in Tennessee was Smiley Hollow, a rustic corporate retreat and working farm located north of downtown Nashville. Nestled in the rolling hills of Goodlettsville, Smiley Hollow provided the perfect location to create the film's exterior concert sequences as well as the supper club musical performances and dance numbers. Production designer Hanania and her crew worked for weeks to transform the retreat's two key locations for the film. This included the retreat's wooden meeting hall to serve as the Meadows Hall supper club where Robby Ray, Miley and Taylor Swift perform during an open mic fundraiser to save Crowley Meadows from a developer.*

138

Outside the Meadows Hall location was the tree-lined expanse of fields where Hanania and her team created the Crowley Meadows farm and site of the "Save the Meadows" fundraiser. Her team constructed a barn, waterwheel, concert stage, carnival booths and rides. More than 2,000 extras filled the Smiley Hollow location, where both Hannah Montana and Miley Stewart perform several of the film's musical numbers, including "Rock Star," "The Climb" and "You'll Always Find Your Way Back Home."

Other Tennessee locations include:

The Belk shoe department in Cool Springs Galleria.

Columbia, TN town square was transformed into the town of "Crawley's Corner" and Franklin High School became "Seaview High School".

The Grand Ballroom of the Hermitage Hotel was featured in a press conference scene.

Miley and Travis have a picnic and a swim at Rutledge Falls in Tullahoma, TN.

Maury Country Regional Airport was also used.

The farm is a private dairy farm only a few miles away from the Cyrus' real-life ranch in Thompson Station, TN.

HEE HAW

In the summer of 1969, CBS unveiled a replacement show for the *Smothers Brothers Comedy Hour* called *Hee Haw*, a unique *Laugh-In*-style sketch program that proved that the Country genre could either be laughed at...or that it had its own sense of humor. After 2 years on CBS, *Hee Haw* moved onto syndication, where it became a household name on TV for 25 seasons. Cast members included legendary names like Buck Owens and Roy Acuff, as well as made TV stars out of Lula Roman, Grandpa Jones, Roy Clark, Minnie Pearl, and countless others. Every week featured a musical guest who would join the house bands, the Buckaroos or the Hee Haw Band (depending on which era), for a few performances, as well as join in the fun in the skits. You can currently tune into RFD-TV to see reruns and relive the heads popping out of the cornfields with their "corny" one-liners. Cornfield...corny joke...get it? You can thank *Hee Haw* for that one.

A number of seasons were filmed at the current WTVF News Channel 5 facility downtown (474 James Robertson Parkway) before they moved production to the Grand Ole Opry house at Opryland, which has a sound stage in the building behind the main theater. Many scenes from the ABC show, *Nashville*, are filmed on the same Opryland sound stage.

HONKY TONK MAN

The near-climax of this Clint Eastwood film has Red and Whit pull up and park outside the 5th Avenue entrance of the Ryman Auditorium, immediately followed by Red singing on-stage inside. This film also marks the final appearance of Marty Robbins.

THE LAST CASTLE

The central yard of the Tennessee State Prison is the primary location for this entire movie, with separate towers, stone pylons, and an entirely fake gothic façade on the front face of the building built specifically for the movie.

LAST DANCE

Once again, the Tennessee State Prison is the natural choice for any film about a woman on death row and needing a foreboding prison backdrop. Bomar Blvd. running along the southwest angle of the front grass makes it's appearance in both "Last Dance" as well as "The Last Castle" when the transport busses arrive at the jail.

The trailer park is at 1326 Dickerson Pike, next to Charlie Bob's, 4th trailer in the north row.

The Tennessee State Capital building and the adjacent mall across Charlotte Avenue are prominently shown in a number of scenes.

THE MATRIX

The opening of "The Matrix" shows Trinity and her would-be assassins running along rooftops, jumping from building to building. While the buildings themselves are based in Sydney, Australia, the cityscape behind her is unmistakably the Nashville skyline. Note the WKDF neon as well as the ears of the Batman Building chopped off to keep from being too recognizable.

NASHVILLE (MOVIE)

While much of the Nashville landscape has changed since Robert Altman and Jerry Weintraub set out to capture the spectacle of Nashville in this epic film, a few locations are still recognizable. The opening scene has a van pulling out of what was then the election headquarters and what is now the front door of the Wildhorse Saloon before looping around and pulling left onto Broadway from 4th Ave. The Nashville Airport makes an appearance, long before numerous renovations. The traffic jam occurs on westbound I-24 just north of the Shelby Street Bridge, in front of the old Continental Inns Of America, now a Ramada Inn. The Nashville Speedway at the Fairgrounds, (where Fan Fair used to take place) is the setting for a comical scene where singers try to sing over the raging motors. The impressive stained glass in the initial church scene is located at St. Henry Catholic Church at 6401 Harding Pike.

A number of popular music venues were used in the film: The Old Time Picking Parlor formerly at 121 2nd Ave N. has a jam session while Deemen's Den, which was once located at the southwest corner of Broadway & 4th Ave (where Merchants currently is), shows up for a scene. The King Of The Road club makes a brief appearance in all its red-velveted glory as does the Exit/In, which looked a little different back in the day with its floor seating and citrus mural of a guitar behind the stage. The brand new (at the time) Grand Ole Opry House and Opryland itself both make a very obvious appearance.

The so-called climax of the movie takes place in front of the Parthenon where a political rally-turned-chaos occurs with the assassination of Barbara Jean. This is no doubt the best location of the film to visit as the park and the Parthenon look essentially the same today as they did during filming.

142

NASHVILLE (TV SERIES)

The first few seasons of ABC's hit show featured recurrent on-location filming at the following locations:

4104 Hillsboro Pike - Bluebird Café

Shelby Street Bridge

1358 Page Rd – Teddy & Rayna's house

619 Boscobel St – Deacon's house

623 Boscobel St – Scarlett and Avery's house

Post Rd & Hill Place Dr. - Gate for Juliette's neighborhood

5125 Annesway Dr. – Juliette's old house

917 Overton Lea Rd – Juilette's new house

565 Brick Church Park Dr. – interior soundstage

231 6th Ave N - Capitol Grille

2804 Opryland Dr. - Grand Ol Opry House

1006 Forrest Ave - The 5 Spot

750 Cowan St - Soundcheck

1107 17th Ave S – South Circle Records

Granny White & Battlefield – Rayna's accident

NE corner of Polk & Church - Highway 65 Records

110 S 17th St - Gunnar's house

Numerous other locations were used for random scenes, including:

RCA Studio A, Catch This Music (1008 17th Ave S.), Broken Spoke, Schermerhorn Symphony Hall, the Roundabout, the Miller Harris Building, Watermark, Jack's Bar-B-Q, Legato Gelato, Belle Meade United Methodist Church, Major Bob Music, Two Old Hippies, Ocean Way Studios, Suntrust Plaza, the Parthenon, Pinnacle building, Leipers Fork Market (4348 Hillsboro Rd, Franklin) and many others.

PERCY JACKSON AND THE OLYMPIANS

Filmmakers of "Percy Jackson & the Olympians: The Lightning Thief" took advantage of the full-scale replica of Athena inside the Parthenon in Centennial Park (and the park itself) for the battle scene where the trio fights the Hydra. A visit to the Parthenon will reveal that the real statue is covered in gold leafing while the "movie-statue" is white and posed differently. However, much of the main room is recognizable from the giant bronze doors to the double-tier of pillars.

STOKER

This much anticipated Nicole Kidman drama was filmed at locations throughout Nashville. Most recognizable is Hillsboro High School standing in for Middle Bend HS at 3812 Hillsboro. The site of "Rocket's Grille" is actually Karin's Kustard at 470 S. Lowry St in Smyrna, TN. And the house featured prominently throughout the film is one of a few at 101 Hillwood Blvd, off of Hwy 70.

SWEET DREAMS

This controversial Patsy Cline biopic had its fair share of filming all around Nashville, with its most recognizable location being the stage of the Ryman Auditorium.

The white "dream house" that was featured in the film is at 6573 Rolling Fork Drive. The real house that Patsy lived in is located at 815 Nella Drive near Goodlettsville.

145

THE THING CALLED LOVE

While a vast amount of the film was shot in Los Angeles (the drive-in, the barn party, the cow-tipping, walking the streets at night, Trisha Yearwood's house, the police station, the music studios, their cabin that is supposedly at Shelby Ave & S 3rd St in East Nashville), there were many key moments of the film that were on location in Nashville.

The most recognizable site is the Bluebird Café, which had it's real exterior and parking lot heavily featured. The interior shots were filmed at Paramount in LA.

The Greyhound station that Miranda arrives at in Nashville is used to be at 8th and Demonbreun where the Convention Center now stands.

The rooms of the Drake Motel are characters in themselves with Miranda's "Disco Room" (#108 in movie, #107 in real life and commemorated with the plaque designating it the "Thing Called Love Room" - although it looks more like #108 in real life) and Linda Lou's "Gone With The Wind" room is #127 but whose interior, unfortunately, was built in LA.

Blakey's Diner across from the Drake Motel does not exist and was built specifically for the movie in a vacant lot across the street.

Miranda's pounding-the-pavement montage takes us through a Music Row tour of S1 Music (65 Music Sq E), the
146

Music Mill which now is home to NSAI (1710 Roy Acuff Place), and the Riverfront at 1st and Broadway, a ways away from the Row downtown.

The scene where Miranda and James are shouting the traditional "Look out Music City 'cuz I'm here now and I ain't never leaving!" is supposed to take place on the roof of the fictional Nashville General Hospital but in actuality, was filmed on the roof of Rolling Mill Hill lofts at 210 Middleton St.

Elvis' barber is located at the northwest corner of Broadway & 2nd (where Cotton Eyed Joe's is now) across the street from the Hard Rock Café, whose parking lot is where the girls pow-wow after Linda Lou's meltdown.

NOT IN NASHVILLE: The mini-mart by Graceland where Miranda and James get married is actually Pat's Liquor Market at 6020 Kester Ave, Van Nuys CA.

NOT IN NASHVILLE: Kyle's auto accident upon hearing Trisha Yearwood sing his song on the radio happens in downtown Los Angeles, starting at 508 Mateo St and ending with the collision in front of Cleveland Art at 110 N. Santa Fe Ave, just north of the East 1st St overpass.

Miranda's bus ride back to NY is interesting as starts on Demonbreun, heads down Hillsboro Pike past the high school, u-turns and heads back UP Hillsboro so that the Bluebird is now on the right, heads over to Murfreesboro Pike in the center turn lane, and then takes a pee break at the Halfway House Café in Santa Clarita, CA. No wonder Greyhound tickets are so expensive these days.

WALK THE LINE

The most recognizable Nashville location in "Walk The Line" is easily the Tennessee State Prison (surprise!), which stands in for the infamous Folsom Prison. The intro scenes show the east gate of the prison and then pan across the yard that was so prominent in the "The Last Castle". The vast majority of the rest of the movie was filmed in and around Memphis and Arkansas.

GRAVES

Not only do famous people write, record, and live in Nashville, but they also die here too. Here are some memorial parks with a few notable interees. Some of these cemeteries have a guide map available in the main office while others might take a little necessary searching. When it comes to cemeteries, what you discover along the way is often more enlightening than what you find when you arrive.

CALVARY CEMETERY
1001 Lebanon Rd, Nashville

Eddie Rabbitt

FOREST LAWN MEMORIAL GARDENS

1150 S. Dickerson Rd, Goodlettsville

David "Stringbean" Akeman
Cowboy Copas
Lefty Frizzell
Hawkshaw Hawkins
Randy Hughes
Irby Mandrell

HARPETH HILLS MEMORIAL GARDENS

9090 Highway 100, Nashville

Chet Atkins
Charlie Louvin
Ira Louvin
Donna Summer

HENDERSONVILLE MEMORIAL GARDENS
353 East Main St, Hendersonville

Johnny Cash
June Carter Cash
Maybelle Carter
Merle Kilgore

THE HERMITAGE
4580 Rachel's Lane, Hermitage

Andrew Jackson
Rachel Jackson

HERMITAGE MEMORIAL GARDENS
535 Shute Lane, Old Hickory

Ernest Tubb

LUTON'S UNITED METHODIST CHURCH
8363 Old Springfield Pike, Goodlettsville

Grandpa Jones

MOUNT HOPE CEMETERY
608 Mount Hope St, Franklin

Minnie Pearl (listed as Sarah Ophelia Colley Cannon)

MT. OLIVET CEMETERY
1101 Lebanon Pike, Nashville

Benjamin Franklin Cheatham (Civil War Confederate Major General)
Cornelia Clark Fort (aviation pioneer)
Vern Gosdin
David Lipscomb
Randall McGavock (Confederate Army Officer)
John Overton

152

Fred Rose
Tootsie Ross
Thomas Ryman

MOUNT VIEW CEMETERY
209 Mountain St, McMinnville

Dottie West

NASHVILLE CITY CEMETERY
1001 4th Ave S, Nashville

Harlan Howard
General James Robertson

SPRING HILL CEMETERY
5110 Gallatin Pike, Nashville

Roy Acuff
Floyd Cramer
Pete Drake
Earl Scruggs
Hank Snow
Billy Walker
Keith Whitley

SUMNER MEMORIAL GARDENS
420 Albert Gallatin Rd, Gallatin

Conway Twitty (Harold Jenkins)

TENNESSEE STATE CAPITOL GROUNDS
600 Charlotte Ave, Nashville

James Polk
Sarah Polk

155

WOODLAWN MEMORIAL
660 Thompson Lane, Nashville

Eddie Arnold
Rob Bironas
Owen Bradley
Boudleaux and Felice Bryant (cross mausoleum)
Little Jimmy Dickens (cross mausoleum)
Kerby Farrell (baseball player)
Dobie Gray
George Jones
Johnny Paycheck (paid for by George Jones)
Webb Pierce
James Percy Priest
Marty Robbins
Jerry Reed (Hubbard) (cross mausoleum)
Dan Seals
Richard Allen Sisler (baseball player)
Van Stephenson (cross mausoleum)
Porter Wagoner
Tammy Wynette (as Virginia Richardson) (cross mausoleum)

FOOD

Kansas City has barbeque, Salt Lake City has garlic burgers, Chicago has hot dogs...but unfortunately Nashville does not have it's own one-of-a-kind-Music-City cuisine. Luckily, it does have some excellent food that cannot be missed! Most of these restaurants have been on the Nashville map for years and if they haven't yet, no doubt one day will be.

BROWNS DINER

2102 Blair Blvd.
www.BrownsDiner.com

Perhaps no restaurant is as much of a Nashville establishment as Brown's Diner is. Nestled in a quaint...er, cozy...umm...ok, let's face it, this place is a dive. But it is a true Nashville tradition and the definitive burger of choice (and Frito pie!) for generations of locals past, present, and future.

CHRISTIE COOKIE COMPANY

1205 3rd Ave N.
www.ChristieCookies.com

If you've ever checked into a Doubletree Hotel, you've no doubt received one of their special treats at the front desk: the coveted Doubletree cookie! This mouthwatering goodie is the recipe of Nashville's own Christie Cookie Company, located on 3rd Street, north of downtown in Germantown. For the past 30 years, Christie Cookie has been mixing up handcrafted quality baked goods with flavors like Snickerdoodle, Lemon White Chocolate, Chocolate Macadamia, and of course, the Doubletree cookie. Stop in to see what's available and to grab a tub to bake at home!

ELLISTON PLACE SODA SHOP

2111 Elliston Place

You've probably seen the Elliston Place Soda Shop and don't even know it. It's retro disposition make it the poster-child for simpler times: when you could split a coke at the fountain with your best girl or guy, when everybody treated you like family in restaurant, and the banana pudding was amazing.

Luckily, that spirit is still alive and well at the Soda Shop, which makes it the perfect location to travel back in time and enjoy those good ol' days. Not only does it serve up a classic array of burgers, shakes, fries, and an awesome

 breakfast, but it's popular in music videos from artists such as Carrie Underwood, Reba McEntire, and Marty Stuart. LeAnn Rimes "worked" there in the network special, "I Get That A Lot". Al Gore announced his running mate to Tom Brokaw at the Soda Shop in 2000. It's featured on the Hank Williams Jr. album cover "One Night Stand" and is also a location for the Tammy Wynette/George Jones movie, "Stand By Your Man". Most recently, it was the diner used in the Farm Bureau commercial that shows a father trying to answer his daughter's tough questions...and gets a little help from Farmer Charlie feeding him answers from the adjacent booth.

And no classic locale would be complete with its hauntings. Supposedly, the Soda Shop's late great cook, Carl, makes himself known to the waitresses as they close the restaurant every now and then. And the Elliston Place Sola Shop's most famous waitress, Jean, still eerily watches over the place from her portrait on the back wall.

LOVELESS CAFE

8400 Tennessee 100, Nashville TN 37221
www.LovelessCafe.com

The Loveless Café is nearly as much of a Nashville landmark as Tootsie's or perhaps even the Ryman Auditorium. Lon and Annie Loveless started the café as a stop for weary travelers of Highway 100, who would recharge with some fried chicken and biscuits in the Loveless' front yard. That same down-home tradition still continues today. Even the famous biscuit recipe has been passed between former and new owners and was famously guarded by the "Biscuit Lady", Carol Fay Ellison, who became the well-deserving face of the Loveless Café before her passing in 2010. If you want to experience a "Mecca" of country cooking in its most traditional setting, come early to get a seat...it really might not get any better than the Loveless Café.

PANCAKE PANTRY

1796 21St Ave S.
www.ThePancakePantry.com

Tourists flock by the hundreds every weekend to taste the legend that is the Pancake Pantry. Locals enjoy it as well, only we know enough to go on a weekday. Expect lines, expect a minimalist approach to the interior, but also expect an unforgettable selection of pancakes and other breakfast items. You won't have to worry about a line the next time you go...you'll be the first one in it.

PATTERSON HOUSE
1711 Division St
www.ThePattersonHouseNashville.com

The coolest spot to see and be seen in Nashville is, no doubt, the Patterson House. Patterson House has brought back the "speakeasy", complete with rules of the establishment (no cell phones, gentlemen do not approach the dames unless invited, etc), an army of bartenders who appear to come straight from their day jobs as band members of Maroon 5, and simply the most laid-back vibe in town. Not only is there a completely unique and original drink list with delicious bitters and liqueurs (bacon whiskey?!) as well as food menu items that have been featured on *Best Thing I Ever Ate* (the Elvis Panini), but you can often have your fair

share of celebrity sightings, putting you right there in the 1940's Hollywood. This author once sat no more that 7 feet from Jack White and Robert Plant discussing their crabgrass issues (at least that's what I imagined) while enjoying a drink at the Patterson House.

Word of warning: dress *more* than appropriately. And be cool, dawg.

THE PHARMACY

731 McFerrin Ave
www.ThePharmacyNashville.com

The Pharmacy is by no means a time-honored Nashville culinary tradition...but this author truly hopes it becomes one. Not only does it have the best burger in town but it's retro ambiance, unique phosphates, and unbeatable beer garden make The Pharmacy a "can't miss" experience. Go!

PRINCE'S HOT CHICKEN SHACK

123 Ewing Dr. #3

Prince's Hot Chicken Shack delivers exactly what is says: very hot chicken in a shack. It has been around as long as anyone can remember, has been featured on *Diners, Drive-Ins, and Dives*, and is considered by locals to be the benchmark of the local delicacy of hot chicken. Be warned though: Prince's Hot Chicken can  be a painful experience to the novice. Plan your meal and the rest of your day accordingly.

ROTIERS

2413 Elliston Place
www.RotiersRestaurant.com

Between the Elliston Place Soda Shop, the Exit/In, and Centennial Park, a visitor could spent all day in this half-mile stretch of Elliston. If you do, you're going to want to eat at Rotier's. Specializing in their cheeseburger on French bread,  which has made countless "Best of Nashville" lists since the beginning of time, it is in constant competition with Brown's Diner to have the best local, hand-packed burger. Ever had a burger on French bread?! Seriously...try it.

FOODIE ALERT! These Nashville restaurants have been featured on the following television shows:

$40 A DAY WITH RACHAEL RAY

Bongo Java – 2007 Belmont Blvd
F. Scott's Restaurant – 2210 Crestmoor Rd
Legend's Corner – 428 Broadway
Provence Breads and Café – 1705 21st Ave S

BEST THING I EVER ATE

Hog Heaven – 115 N. 27th Ave
Patterson House – 1711 Division St
Raz'z Bar & Grill – 2241 Murfreesboro Pk

DINERS, DRIVE-INS, AND DIVES

Arnold Country Kitchen – 605 Eighth Ave S
Athens Family Restaurant – 2526 Franklin Pk
Bro's Cajun Cuiside – 3214 Charlotte Ave
Café Nonna – 4427 Murphy Rd
Café Rakka – 71 New Shackle Island Rd #A,
Hendersonville
Grilled Cheeserie – mobile food truck
Jamaica Way – 900 8th Ave N
Martin's BBQ Joint – 7215 Nolensville Rd
Mas Tacos Por Favor – 732 McFerrin Ave
Phat Bites – 2730b Lebanon Pike
Savarino's Cucina – 2121 Belcourt Ave

DRINKING MADE EASY

12 South Taproom & Grill – 2312 12 Ave S
City House – 1222 4th Ave N
No. 308 – 407 Gallatin Ave
Patterson House – 1711 Division St
Whiskey Kitchen – 118 12th Ave S

EAT STREET

I Dream of Weenie – 1108 Woodland Ave

FOOD PARADISE

Bolton's Spicy Chicken – 624 Main St
Pancake Pantry – 1796 21st Ave S
Prince's Hot Chicken Shack – 123 Ewing Dr #3

MAN FINDS FOOD

Gabby's Burgers – 493 Humphreys St
Masons – 2100 West End Ave
Pinewood Social – 33 Peabody St

THROWDOWN WITH BOBBY FLAY

Las Paletas – 2911 12th Ave S
Loveless Café – 8400 TN 100

THE SONGS

"So, as you can see, even though the location seems to have had some fairy dust on it, the inspiration for these songs were all seeded in some prior location or event that had little or nothing to do with where they were actually written. It was just one more room with bare walls and thankfully, a window. As I recall, the main inspiration for writing songs back then was the same as it is now for the most part: groceries and rent. I even recall certain writers at the time telling me they had concocted stories about the writing of certain hits to make them sound more interesting in the press. Not to say there haven't been songs with inspiring stories behind them. I often wonder when I hear of one though, is it true? And more importantly, does it matter?"
~Chuck Jones

It is estimated that over a thousand songs are written in Nashville every day: the girl holed up in a rented duplex just down the street...the guy scrawling on his smartphone over in the corner...the writers kicking ideas back and forth in an anonymous room on Music Row. These are daily scenarios in Music City. Nashville is the place to come to not only learn how to write but how to co-write...to sit in a room with a stranger, bare your soul, and create a masterpiece that everyone in the world can relate to. Oh, and it's has to be up-tempo and positive! So where do the songs get written? This section is a very, very, very short list of a few recognizable hits and where they were created. There will always be a debate on inspiration of a song: "Where did you get the idea?!" is the most popular question for songwriters. Here, we answer the question, "Where did you write it?!"

ACHY BREAKY HEART – BILLY RAY CYRUS
Don Von Tress

1710 Roy Acuff Place

"Achy Breaky Heart" was an experiment in writing by Don Von Tress who had been told that his writing up to that point was too deep, epic, and intellectual. On one of his subsequent trips to Nashville, Don brought Russ Zavitson, who was running the publishing company at the Music Mill, a first verse and Chorus of a song he was calling "Don't Tell My Heart". Everyone in the office got a pretty good kick out of it so Russ told him to go across the upstairs hall and finish it up, which Don did in 30 minutes or so. They immediately began pitching it around town to some very mixed emotions.

Russ Zavitson:
"I've never seen anything like it in my life, ever. I mean, people either loved it or hated it. It got to the point that I started getting calls from A&R people saying 'Don't play this

song for any of our artists anymore...we absolutely hate this song'. It's goofy...the whole thing is a joke: 'Or tell your brother Cliff...whose fist could tell my lip...tell your dog to bite my leg.' But we all got it. If some idiot says 'Hey, don't tell my heart...my achy breaky heart', it's not funny! But it's that deadpan approach from somebody you don't expect it from...that's what it was for us."

The song eventually got cut a few times: Roger Marshall, Charlie Floyd, and the Marcy Brothers (and almost Ronnie Milsap as well as the Oak Ridge Boys) all had versions laid down for various projects. But it wasn't until a new act on Mercury named Billy Ray Cyrus made the newly-titled "Achy Breaky Heart" a worldwide #1 phenomenon that continues to make its way into daily pop culture.

Zavitson: "I think the song is brilliant and even to this day, I'd love to have another one. People started beating him up over it but, I gotta tell you, I thought the lyric was brilliant. I laughed all the way through it. In my humble estimation as a song publisher, I just thought it was absolutely perfect.

AIN'T GOING DOWN (TIL THE SUN COMES UP) – GARTH BROOKS
Garth Brooks/Kent Blazy/Kim Williams

1026 Overton Lea

This was the first song the trio had written on the back porch of Kent's new house. With Kent spitting out lyrics, Kim strumming the guitar, and Garth pacing back and forth, they wanted to write something fun...and also something

171

that was so subtly dirty that radio wouldn't actually know it was dirty.

ALONE WITH YOU – JAKE OWEN
Writers: Shane Mcanally/JT Harding/Catt Gravitt

1604 17th Ave S

Shane McAnally: "Alone With You" was written in the XIX Building in this tiny room upstairs that has an old keyboard and a giant old TV in it. There is this cushion that sits in the window, and I was sitting there trying to re-create the magic of "Somewhere With You" with JT Harding and Catt Gravitt. JT and I had just found out that "Somewhere With You" was gonna be Kenny Chesney's next single, so we were fired up to write a song in the same vein. The room was/is tiny. I have written a handful of songs in that room, and it feels like a teenager's bedroom. The ceiling is low, and it gets smaller

everytime I'm in it, but there is a magic about it. I have written some of my favorite songs there. We started with a lyric that I had stolen from the title of a book: "you've got me running with scissors". For about 2 hours, the song was called "running with scissors". Ironically, that lyric was changed when Jake Owen recorded the song. Anyway, we had the entire song written and work taped, and we were ready to head home, when Catt said she didn't think the chorus hit hard enough, and that we needed more sex. Next came the re-write and the line "don't slip your hand under my shirt..."

ANYTHING GOES – RANDY HOUSER

Brice Long/John Wiggins

1605 Horton Ave condos

Brice Long: "Anything Goes" was started in a condo on Horton Ave then finished a few weeks later at my house in Springfield, TN.. I was out on a radio tour when I was signed at Sony and came in for one day...I think it was a Wednesday. John and I got together that day at his condo on Horton and wrote first verse, chorus, and most of second verse. Then a few weeks later, maybe a month or more, John was moving and found the work tape we had made when we started it.

He called me and told me to listen to what we had started and I was knocked out. So we got together and finished the song...the rest is what you hear when Randy sings it! ~BL

CADILLAC RANCH – CHRIS LEDOUX

Chuck Jones/Chris Waters

Inspired: Cadillac Ranch outside Amarillo, TX
Written: 10 Music Circle S.

Chuck Jones: "As I recall, Chris Waters and I were in the front room upstairs, the entire outside wall being a window that looked out onto the street. Across the street from us was the parking lot behind what was then CBS Records, originally the famed Quonset Hut Studio. Working with Chris was always interesting and fun. He was, and is, an actual Rhodes scholar.

I had written the title down as a result of having traveled past the actual 'Cadillac Ranch' (in Amarillo, TX) several times in my early twenties. Mostly going to and from California, either hitch hiking or driving an old Chevy van. One impetus for the song was the fact that American farmers had fallen on hard times back then. This was when Willy Nelson's Farm Aid was just coming into it's own. All the  small farms were being foreclosed on, probably as a result of not being able to compete with the corporate farmers. That and the fact that many had borrowed heavily and simply couldn't repay their loans. Regardless, there was a lot of sympathy for the plight of the small American farmer in those days, and Chris and I thought that a song about one such family taking a different approach to their problems would be funny and entertaining. And of course, we had to get an actual Cadillac in there somewhere. So, in the bridge, the implication is that their new approach to farming, raising 'Caine', has yielded  them enough success to get 'em a vintage Cadillac."

CAN'T BE REALLY GONE - TIM MCGRAW

Gary Burr

1106 17th Ave S

Written in this
building when Gary
Burr had his office
here.

DID YOU KNOW:
CEDARWOOD PUBLISHING

39 Music Sq. E

Founded by Webb Pierce and Jim Denny, Cedarwood was
the first publishing company to set up shop on Music Row. It
one also of the most influential Country publishing houses in
Nashville before it was absorbed into Tree Publishing.
Denny was a former WSM employee, venturing into the
world of publishing, booking, and promotion, all of which
helped the Nashville music explosion of the late '50s. He and
Pierce founded Cedarwood in this building right across the
street from the Quonset
Hut and was frequented by
Owen Bradley and his
artists looking for hits.
More importantly, it wasn't
long before Webb began a
string of #1 hits published
by Cedarwood, catapulting
the company into success.

Denny then signed a few house writers such as Mel Tillis, Red Sovine, and an up-and-comer by the name of Buddy Holley.

Denny has another interesting footnote: he personally delivered Buddy Holley his new recording contract with Decca Records in which the "e" in "Holley" had inadvertently been left out due to a typo. Buddy was too scared that Decca would cancel the contract if he complained so he went along with it and "Buddy Holly" history was made.

CHASIN' THAT NEON RAINBOW – ALAN JACKSON
Jim McBride/Alan Jackson

35 Music Sq E., 3rd floor

Before Alan Jackson became a household name and was still developing as an artist, he would frequently write with Jim McBride, a veteran writer with a number of classic hits to his name. This song came about as Alan was venting his frustrations of his musical journey...and dreaming about better days to come. According to McBride, they wrote it in  an upstairs room that was so hot, they had to prop open the door for ventilation. The box they used to prop it was full of awards given to and forgotten by Kris Kristofferson.

CHATTAHOOCHEE – ALAN JACKSON

Jim McBride/Alan Jackson

1812 Lombardy Ave

The idea came from an Exxon Travel magazine featuring an article on the Chattahoochee River that Jim McBride was reading upstairs in his office at this address.

Jim McBride: "I read the article and I thought 'Man, that's kinda cool!' I'd remembered 'Song Of The Chattahoochee' from high school English. I don't know why but I put the magazine down and I started coming up with ideas...the next thing I knew, I was singing 'Way down yonder on the Chattahoochee, it gets hotter than a hoochie coochie.'"

While the first couple of lines were written here, he and Alan Jackson finished it up in Thibadeax, LA where Alan worked it up for sound check and performed it at the show that night.

COME OVER – KENNY CHESNEY
Josh Osborne/Shane McAnally/Sam Hunt

12 Music Circle South

"Come Over" was written in the upstairs Black River conference room back when the whole company was housed in the admin building. Sam Hunt came in with the verse melody already laid out but didn't have any lyrics so he, Josh, and Shane just threw some "filler" lines in here and there, a number of which just seemed to fit and ended up in the final version. The repetitive vamp of "come over, come over, come over, come over" didn't lock in until nearly the end of the song when Sam was randomly vamping in the outro. The catchy repetition caught everyone's attention and they immediately slid that in as the actual chorus. Essentially, this song was written backwards, with melody first, main lyric next, and the title being the final missing piece.

CRAZY – PATSY CLINE
Willie Nelson

422 Broadway - Tootsie's Orchid Lounge

It is known and confirmed that Willie Nelson once lived in the apartments above Tootsie's Orchid Lounge and that he was a regular at the bar. But a favorite urban legend of Broadway that lives on is that Willie wrote the classic

"Crazy" at the front table of the bar. Let's put this one in the "We wish it were true!" category...but unfortunately, Willie wrote "Crazy" on one of his many Texas road trips. So many tourists are told that story that it must be true by now,

even if it wasn't. It *is* true, however, that Willie pitched the song to Patsy's husband, Charlie Dick, in Tootsie's and it was one of the first ones he officially "sold" for a major cut.

THE DANCE - GARTH BROOKS
Tony Arata

255 Summit Ridge Dr

Tony Arata: "The apartment was built like a light house (4 floors) and I used to hang out in the laundry room which was all the way at the bottom; concrete floors and no frills. "The Dance" was the first song I wrote when we moved to town. I will never forget the night that Garth picked me up at Douglas Corner and brought me over to hear the final mixes on his first album. When I heard what he, Allen Reynolds, and Mark Miller and the musicians created from that scratchy guitar/vocal demo, I was reminded why they call some folks 'artists'."

179

DIXIE CHICKEN – LITTLE FEAT
Lowell George/Fred Martin

2613 West End Ave.

In the song, "Dixie Chicken", the band Little Feat refers to the Commodore Hotel in Memphis. Unfortunately, there's never been a Commodore Hotel in Memphis. But Little Feat did stop through Nashville quite a bit around the time this song was written and allegedly frequented a bar in their hotel named, ironically, the Commodore Lounge. Coincidence? Hey, legends have to start somewhere, right?

DRUNK LAST NIGHT – ELI YOUNG BAND
Josh Osborne/Laura Veltz

10 Music Circle South (*see "Cadillac Ranch" for photo*)

Written in the same rooms that a number of historical classic hits were, "Drunk Last Night" was pieced together upstairs in the Black River publishing building. The co-write was supposed to be Josh, Laura, and Trevor Rosen but Trevor ended up having to miss the session...so Josh and Laura got to work on an idea by themselves. According to Josh, Laura had come in with a separate and more "worldly" idea that they chipped away at for awhile. A little while in, Laura went to grab some coffee and mentioned that she might not be the best person to write that worldly song with because she

180

"got a little drunk last night". Josh heard and loved how that rolled off her tongue and said "THAT'S the song that we need to write today!". Eli Young Band took the song to #1.

*Author's Note: Look up "Cecilia" & "The Veltz Family" for some incredible music from Laura Veltz' family band from back in the day – I've been a fan of theirs since the early 2000's and they have a phenomenal catalog of some crazy good music.

EL PASO – MARTY ROBBINS
Marty Robbins

713 18th Ave S

Marty Robbins had his private office in the attic of this building and was the room where he wrote a vast number of hits, allegedly including his standard, "El Paso".
And when you're in the real El Paso, be sure to stop by the real Rosa's Cantina at 3454 Doniphan Drive.

FACE TO FACE – GARTH BROOKS
Tony Arata

255 Summit Ridge Dr *(see "The Dance" for photo)*

Tony Arata: "The apartment was built like a light house (4 floors) and I used to hang out in the laundry room which was all the way at the bottom; concrete floors and no frills. "Here

I Am" and "Face to Face" were both written early in the morning before I used to go load trucks at UPS."

FOOL HEARTED MEMORY – GEORGE STRAIT
Byron Hill/Blake Mevis

1217 16th Ave S

Byron Hill (from his website, ByronHillMusic.com):"The song 'Fool Hearted Memory' was written in 1981 in a small, upstairs, southwest corner room at 1217 16th Avenue South in Nashville, which is the building where my publisher... ATV Music's offices were. I had recently written and produced a track for the movie 'The Exterminator', and the same production company came back to me for another song for another movie called 'The Soldier'. Thanks to ATV Music's Gerry Teifer (my publisher) and MCA Records' Jim Foglesong, and producer Blake Mevis, a deal was done that included giving a young new MCA recording artist a cameo role in the

movie singing a song that ideally could be on his album and on the soundtrack album, and a potential hit single. That new MCA artist was George Strait, and he was a perfect match for the movie and the song. I co-wrote the song with Blake Mevis, and 'Fool Hearted Memory' became a historic first number one record for George Strait and my first number one as a songwriter. In 1981, Strait had debuted at #6 with "Unwound." He followed that up with a single that went to #15 called "Down and Out," then charted to #3 with "If You're Thinking You Want a Stranger, finally scoring his first

#1 hit with his fourth release "Fool Hearted Memory" on August 28, 1982. The song won an ASCAP Award for being one of the most performed country songs of 1982."
~BH

FRIENDS IN LOW PLACES – GARTH BROOKS
Earl Bud Lee/Dewayne Blackwell

26 Music Sq E. – Idea
204 21st Ave S. – Lyrics
1906 Chet Atkins Pl. – Music

The original idea for the line "friends in low places" came from a lunch at the old Tavern On The Row restaurant (26 Music Sq. E) where Bud and Dewayne were hanging out with a group of friends. Someone asked who was going to pay for the meal, to which Bud replied, "Don't worry. I've got friends in low places…I know the cook!"

Bud and Dewayne rolled the idea around for a full year before finally running into each other at what at the time was O'Charleys (204 21st Ave S) at an event that was serving champagne. Sitting at

183

the bar, less than an hour later, they had the full lyric scrawled on a napkin.

At that point, they still needed music for the song so they went over to DeWayne's apartment at the Americana (1906 Chet Atkins Pl) and used a 3-fret guitar on loan from Harlan Howard himself to map out the chords and melody. Since the guitar only had 3 frets, the writers could not go up the neck in their progressions and could only go down...hence the signature 2nd chord, which makes the song immediately recognizable.

The writers hired an up-and-coming demo singer named Garth Brooks to sing the demo for them, which turned out to be Garth's last demo session ever, as he was about to sign

with Capital Records. He kept the song in mind, though, recorded it on his massive smash album, "No Fences", and released it as a single right after "The Dance", helping secure his place as a music icon.

GEORGIA RAIN – TRISHA YEARWOOD
Karyn Rochelle/Ed Hill

1313 16th Ave S. - Big Yellow Dog upstairs

"Georgia Rain" was originally called "Augusta Rain" when Karyn and Ed first finished it up in an upstairs writing room at Big Yellow Dog. Trisha Yearwood immediately showed interest in the song but requested to change the hook and title not only making it more universal to her home state of

184

Georgia but also because it was sounding a lot like "a gust of rain".

In an article for *American Songwriter* magazine, Karyn says "I really can't explain it, I just knew it was meant for her. Ed agreed and my publisher sent the song over  to her producer. Trisha had taken a few years off at that time but was making a new record. Her producer, Garth Fundis, invited me over to the studio (Sound Emporium) to hear it after they had finished recording it. I sat down at the control board and listened with tears in my eyes. To me, Trisha has the most incredible female voice Nashville has ever heard. To hear her sing the words and melody that I wrote was the most surreal experience ever."

HARPER VALLEY P.T.A. – JEANNIE C. RILEY

Tom T. Hall

7840 Learning Lane

Tom T. Hall liked the name of the elementary school at this location, the Harpeth Valley Elementary School, and used it as inspiration for his classic, *Harper Valley P.T.A.*

HAUNTED HEART – SAMMY KERSHAW
Kim Williams/Buddy Brock

1728 Stokes Lane

Kim Williams: "Buddy Brock & I wrote that song in about an hour at my townhouse at 1728 Stokes Lane. My wife Phyllis and my daughter Amanda lived next door to Kathy Mattea there. The song became the title to one of  Sammy Kershaw's albums and got to #3 on the charts."

HEADED FOR A HEARTACHE – GARY MORRIS
Kent Blazy/Jim Dowell

820 18th Ave S

This is one of Kent Blazy's first hits, written with Jim Dowell back when New Albany Hoosier Music was located here.

HERE I AM – PATTY LOVELESS
Tony Arata

255 Summit Ridge Dr *(see "The Dance" for photo)*

Tony Arata: "The apartment was built like a light house (4 floors) and I used to hang out in the laundry room which was all the way at the bottom; concrete floors and no frills. "Here I Am" and "Face to Face" were both written early in the morning before I used to go load trucks at UPS."

NOT IN NASHVILLE
THE HOUSE THAT BUILT ME – Miranda Lambert
Tom Douglas/Allen Shamblin

If there's one song that every songwriter in recent history will wish they would've or even *could've* written, "The House That Built Me" might be the strongest contender. The song was actually conceived at the Sundance Songwriter Series in Utah, which Tom Douglas and Allen Shamblin were performing at in 2004. Shamblin had recently read an article on houses and how they have their own memories and thought it might make for a good song idea. So the two writers wrote an initial version, finished it up at Tom's house in Nashville, and pitched it around – but for some reason, they didn't get a whole lot of response from it. Every few years, for the next 6 years (aspiring songwriters, take note: *6 years*), they would take a fresh look at it and chip away at any weak spots. It wasn't until they got rid of some unnecessary information in the song and eventually discovered that homerun set up line of "If I could just come in, I swear I'll leave...won't take nothing but a memory...from the house that built me" that it really locked in and seemed to get the emotional response that it was going for. Rumor has it that Blake Shelton was in his truck, listening to a compilation of songs that had been sent to him by his record label, Warner Brothers, when his wife at the time heard this song and said "That's my story!" and started crying. Blake apparently relinquished the song and it became a #1 for Miranda.

I HEAR A CALL – EMMYLOU HARRIS
Tony Arata

3614 Mayflower Place

Tony Arata: "The first home Jaymi and I ever owned. I wrote it as a prayer for my mother. I later added the music and performed it first at one of my nephew's weddings in Jonesboro, GA. Hearing Emmylou sing it was one of the highlights of my musical life."

I LOVE THE WAY YOU LOVE ME – JOHN MICHAEL MONTGOMERY
Victoria Shaw/Chuck Cannon

20 E. Music Circle

Victoria Shaw: "This started out on a drive from New York to a gig in Pennsylvania. I was dating this guy (who I ended up marrying) and I

was thinking about how great he kissed – and that sexy sound a kiss makes. The first 4 or 5 lines, with music, popped in my head, which is very, very rare. I pulled over on the side of the road and called my apartment and sang it into my answering machine. I carried it around for quite awhile until I got together with Chuck Cannon in Nashville."

DID YOU KNOW
I RUN TO YOU – LADY ANTEBELLUM
Tom Douglas/Hillary Scott/Charles Kelley/Dave Haywood

Tom Douglas was running in the Country Music Marathon on a Saturday in 2007 and spent a good number of miles behind a runner whose shirt said "I Run This Town". Like any songwriter would, Tom made a note of all the things in town that the guy could "run" and even chiseled a couple of lines – "I run from hate…I run from prejudice" – before his co-write on Monday, with a new group being developed going by the name of Lady Antebellum. They loved the idea, knocked out the song that day at Tom's house, and it became their first #1.

I WILL ALWAYS LOVE YOU – DOLLY PARTON
Dolly Parton
811 18th Ave S.

Long ago, this building housed the publishing company of OwePar Music, a co-venture between Owen Bradley and Dolly Parton. Porter Wagoner owned this building as well as Fireside Studio next

door and leased this building to OwePar. As Porter and Dolly's relationship began to crumble, Dolly slipped away from Fireside and went next door to this writing refuge and crafted her massive hit, "I Will Always Love You" on the front porch, a song that has brought her well over $25 million over the life of the song. The porch has been enclosed and is now the front reception area. *As this book was going into printing, both this house and the neighboring Fireside Studios were torn down to build an apartment complex.

IF THE DEVIL DANCED – JOE DIFFIE
Kim Williams/Ken Spooner

1100C 17th Ave S

Kim Williams: "It was my first and Joe's first #1. We used the metaphor of the car salesmen and the second time we met, we finished it. I wrote it with Ken Spooner and he saw a two-tone Nash parked near my apartment so we put the car in the song. This was my first #1 song, produced by Bob Montgomery and sung by Joe Diffie, who was already a dear friend from all the demo singing he did for me."

IF TOMORROW NEVER COMES – GARTH BROOKS

Garth Brooks/Kent Blazy

1705 Warfield Dr

Bob Doyle introduced his new artist, Garth Brooks, to Kent Blazy in late 1986 and told them both that they needed to write together. Kent didn't have an open appointment until February 1 of 1987 so they had to wait a little while. When they finally sat down at this house to write, Garth presented Kent with a story line he'd been working on, which seemed to Kent to be more of a 2nd verse of a song. According to legend, Kent then proceeded to spit out the words that he thought would make a pretty good first verse, beginning with "Sometimes late at night..." and thus, Garth's first #1 record was written.

I'M HOLDING MY OWN – LEE ROY PARNELL

Tony Arata

3614 Mayflower Place *(see "I Hear A Call" for photo)*

Tony Arata: "The first time I heard what Lee Roy Parnell and company did to it, I was stunned. It is a big sounding record."

IN PICTURES – ALABAMA

Joe Doyle/Bobby Boyd

1 Music Circle North
1001 Copperstill Ct., Kingston Springs

Joe Doyle: "This song was born after walking into my songplugger Bobby Boyd's office at BMG, located on the 2nd floor of 1 Music Circle North, sometime in 1992. He had a new photo of his son, who I believe lived in Texas, on the window ledge in his office. I remarked, 'That boy is getting big', Bobby's somewhat mournful response was 'Yeah, I'm watching him grow in pictures.' I immediately made a mental note; that sure sounds like a good song idea, but I didn't say anything about it and went about our typical conversation about who knows what.

I soon took a trip back home to Rhode Island to visit with my family and on these visits, I usually stayed with one of my sisters, who had recently begun having children and I thoroughly enjoyed spending time with the little ones. On a flight back to Nashville, I began to think of how sad it would be if they were my own kids and I only got to see them a few times a year, missing out on all their childhood milestones:

first steps, first words and so on. Which of course, led me back to the phrase Bobby had uttered; 'Yeah, I'm watching him grow up in pictures.' The next day I stayed home and sat at the baby grand in the converted garage of our old house in Kingston Springs at 1001 Copperstill Court and the chorus, 'I missed her first steps, her first words and I love you daddy is something I seldom heard, oh it hurts me so to watch my baby grow, up in pictures' just fell out. I remember thinking to myself 'This is a good "verse"'. Shows how much I knew.

The next time I stopped in the office to visit with Bobby, I told him I had used something he had said to me in conversation in a song and had a chorus and some verse ideas mapped out. I politely asked if he didn't mind me using what he had said to me. Over the next week or two I would stop in and ask him what he thought of my latest ideas and we talked about the realities of the situation I was attempting to write about. Once I had finished the song, we cordially agreed that I would retain 2/3 writer's share and Bobby would have 1/3 writer's share for his title.

In a short period of time after demoing the song, Linda Davis recorded a wonderful, heart felt version for her Arista debut CD and as luck would have it, Alabama would hear her version listening to her CD *Shoot for the Moon* while driving the through the Georgia mountains and decided to record it themselves and make it the title track of their 1995 CD release. It would become a #1 Country single in December of '95."

Photo Credit: Lisa Bradley-Doyle

193

KEEPER OF THE STARS – TRACY BYRD
Dickie Lee/Danny Mayo/Karen Staley

8 Music Sq W - Sony ATV Publishing

This Tracy Byrd hit from 1995 is just one of countless many that have been written in this publishing office. Lee and Mayo had been working through the idea, had the title and a few starter lines but were stuck enough to call on Staley to help it find it's magic. The song went on to become the 1995 CMA Song Of The Year.

DID YOU KNOW:
LADY ANTEBELLUM
1600 17th Ave S

Hillary, Charles, and Dave used to hang out, sleep in, write in – essentially live in this building prior to their mainstream success. Hillary had been writing for Victoria Shaw since she was 15 so when Victoria saw Hillary sing with some "new guys she'd met" at the Exit/In, she immediately recognized the talent and began to write with, rehearse, and develop the group in her offices located in the top floor of this building.

LAST CALL – LEE ANN WOMACK
Shane McAnally/Erin Enderlin

1904 Adelicia St, room #6
Universal Publishing

Shane McAnally: "Last Call" was written on Halloween. It had rained all day. Erin Enderlin and I were in room #6 at Universal Publishing on Adelecia in Nashville. I remember everything about the room and the lamps and the oddly shaped couch I was sitting on when Erin sang the words 'I bet you're in a bar'. It stopped me in my tracks. We had already been working on the song for about 3 hours at that point, but had made very little ground. When she sang those words, however, the song wrote itself in another hour. The last piece of the puzzle was the title. We had every other line in the chorus, and somehow the songwriting God's hung in with us that day, and led us straight to the hook: 'I bet you're in a bar, cause I'm always your last call'. We knew it was special. Definitely my favorite Halloween treat of all time. "

LEAVE THE NIGHT ON – SAM HUNT
Josh Osborne/Shane McAnally/Sam Hunt

24 Music Square West

"Leave The Night On" was inspired by an email that Sam misread where someone said "leave the light on" but which he thought said "leave the night on". He brought the idea in to the writing session with Shane and Josh at the Carnival building across from RCA Studio B and they both jumped at it. They got the majority written but still needed some additional color in the chorus, with suggestions being made that they needed something in there similar to how Pat Monahan from Train writes in his lyrics. That sparked the "sky is dropping Jupiter around us like some old train" line and completed the song. "Leave The Night On" became Sam Hunt's first #1 as a solo artist.

LET'S GO TO VEGAS – FAITH HILL
Karen Staley

757 Newberry Rd

Written in 1994, "Let's Go To Vegas" started off as a joke between writer Karen Staley and a few of her friends. Subtly using inspiration from "Fishing In The Dark", she wrote it in about 45 minutes in this house and turned it into her publisher as part of the joke. Faith Hill ended up loving it (Alan Jackson was apparently mad that he didn't get the song first) and making it the lead-off hit from her *It Matters To Me* album. Ironically, Staley was in the Vegas airport when she was told that Faith had recorded the song.

LIKE WE NEVER HAD A BROKEN HEART
– TRISHA YEARWOOD
Garth Brooks/Pat Alger

Jack's Tracks - 1308 16th Ave S

This was one of a number of early collaborations between Brooks and Alger, written here in the upstairs writing room of Jack's Tracks.

NOT IN NASHVILLE:
LITTLE ROCK – COLLIN RAYE
Tom Douglas

Although it's Nashville roots play out a little further in its story, this song was technically written, according to Tom Douglas, in Dallas, TX in the Southern Methodist University music building. Douglas had recently moved back to Texas after giving it a go in Nashville, with absolutely no desire to ever return...until "Little Rock" fell out one Saturday morning at that piano in SMU. Its main message wasn't so much about alcoholism as it was about starting over – a sentiment that Douglas could relate to after his move and he made a specific point to make that message as honest as he could, without any distraction or worry about radio. Fast-forward a few months...Tom goes back to

197

Nashville for Thanksgiving to visit his wife's family and happened to randomly play the song for renown producer and engineer Bill Deaton (coincidentally at a piano at Peabody College at Vandy), who immediately pulled Tom into the Glaser Brothers Studio (**916 19ᵗʰ Ave**) and recorded a demo on the song. A few weeks later, Tom ran into Paul Worley, gave him a copy of the demo, and got signed to Sony. Collin Raye released "Little Rock" in 1994 and scored a #2 with one of the most masterfully written songs in Country Music history.

LOVE A LITTLE STRONGER – DIAMOND RIO

Chuck Jones/Greg Swint/Billy Crittenden

10 Music Circle S

Chuck Jones: "'Love A Little Stronger' was born out of the need for songs for a potential trio, two of the members being my co writers on the song: Greg Swint and Billy Crittenden. Billy had a studio in his basement over off of 12 Ave. He was also a great high harmony singer. When Billy found a financial backer to finance his dream of being a hit country act (he had previously sang backgrounds and gospel), he suggested me to produce them. That's how I

ended up writing with Billy. Greg Swint was to be the lead singer, and he was really quite good. They wanted to be a trio a la Diamond Rio, and they were trying to talk me into being the third guy and low harmony singer. I was having too much success as a writer at the time to think about concentrating on anything else, but I did agree to write heavily with them, help search for a third member, and produce the final product; and to pitch it to the labels as well.

I still remember the day we started 'Love A Little Stronger' quite well. Greg and Billy were great singers, and I've always loved working with great singers. As we wrote the song, they would be working out harmony parts, which was inspiring to me as a lyricist. We were writing specifically for three-part harmony. I think we worked all day and had most of the melody, but only a filler lyric. Long about four p.m., after having gone to a late lunch, we were still singing something like 'Dance a little longer, sing a little louder' for the chorus line. Then something clicked all of the sudden and it occurred to me that the phrase that had been in the back of my head, 'Love A Little Stronger', although a bit trite was actually the perfect hook. After that came, a first verse just fell out in one piece. By that time, someone had to go and so we agreed to get back together and finish it.

It just so happened that Billy's financial backer (who had publishing on Greg, maybe Billy as well), offered to send the three of us, and my wife, on a weeklong trip to the Virgin Islands, specifically St. John, a ferry ride from St. Thomas. She wouldn't be accompanying us, but she rented a nice house for us to stay in. She actually lived in St. Thomas at that time, and her dad was the Ambassador. While vacationing on St. Thomas, we finished the second verse of the song. Now that I'm thinking about it, we might not have had the title until St. John.

It was on this trip that evidence of impending doom regarding the trio first surfaced. Billy and Greg weren't getting along that well when thrown together for extended periods of time. Billy had decided to bow out of the deal. About the time I had the project finished and mixed, the artist, Greg Swint, began to disappear for days at a time. I was flabbergasted that I had invested six months of my life into writing and producing a project only to have one member quit and the other remaining member disappear.

The first I heard about interest in the song from Diamond Rio was the night that Greg and Billy's financial backer called me to tell me it was already recorded and was going to be released as their first single in a couple of weeks, as the title cut of their new record. She had some or all of their publishing on the song and had made a deal with Julie Daniels of Island Bound for Julie to get part of the publishing in return for pitching the song. Julie is the one who got it to Diamond Rio. And I will be forever grateful.

Oh, one more thing about this song: it was written and demoed in third person:

'Love a little stronger, dig a little deeper
Go a little farther, anything to please her
Tonight he's gonna start, show that girl what's in his heart.....'

They never asked if they could change the lyric. The first I knew about it was when someone played me the unreleased record. I heard:

'Love a little stronger, dig a little deeper
Go a little farther, anything to please you girl
Tonight I'm gonna start, show you girl what's in my heart....'

I was actually pissed off at first, but of course, they were right....."

200

LOVE LIKE CRAZY – LEE BRICE
Doug Johnson/Tim James

1815 Division Street

Doug Johnson had a 2nd floor studio in this building where he and Tim James wrote the longest charting song in Billboard history, "Love Like Crazy".

LOVE ME LIKE YOU MEAN IT – KELSEA BALLERINI
Kelsea Ballerini/Lance Carpenter/Josh Kerr/Forest Glen Whitehead

10 Music Circle S (*see "Love A Little Stronger" for photo*)

Lance Carpenter: It was a Monday night, me and Forest Glen Whitehead (my roommate at the time) would write every other Monday and usually leave the house and write at Black River around 7pm...just to get away from our comfort zone and it was usually quiet there. On this particular night we didn't have anything we were working on and Forest mentioned two fairly new Black River writers were hanging out, Josh Kerr and Kelsea Ballerini...we thought it'd be cool to just hang and order pizza...get to know them. Well, get 4 songwriters together and a song is going to break out and it did...but we got a verse chorus into it and Kelsea wasn't feeling it so we backed up and punted to our original plan...order pizza...Soulshine Pizza (Carnivore) to be exact...at least that was what me and Forest got. Pizza showed up around 8pm. Long story short, sitting in the living room area of the BRE offices someone threw out the

201

title "Love Me Like You Mean It" and someone said "kiss me like you need it", and someone said "hold me like i'm leaving"...all jokingly...till we put all of the phrases together and thought hey that's a chorus. Josh or Forest one picked up a guitar and started playing the riffy intro to the song and away we went. Didn't know how easy all 4 of us would be to get back together so we decided to push past 10pm We talked about trying to find a sassy side to Kelsea and so we started listening to Rihanna "Take A Bow" and used that to build the verse mood. Kelsea said "oh hey" and I looked at Josh who was wearing his flat bill hat backwards and said "Oh hey, Josh, got your hat back...Kelsea said "Ooh, I kinda like that!" And the race was on. We finished the song about 12:30am and we finished, work taped the song and thought man that's catchy and simple...but that was our theme the whole night...path of least resistance...we didn't want to overcomplicate it, keep it conversational, simple, and catchy, but real...a few weeks later or a month maybe Forest did a demo and Kelsea sang on it, that afternoon he called me into his studio and said you have to hear this...it was still simple, conversational, and catchy but it sounded like a big ole hit...(granted neither one of us had one of those or knew what they were really) it just sounded right! We played it for our publishers who both loved it but along with us we didn't know who we'd pitch it to because it sounded so different than anything on the radio. Kelsea really does have her own voice...and now everybody knows that. She didn't have a record deal at the time but as the song grew on the label she ended up getting a record deal offer and it was chosen as the first single. Released first to Sirius XM The Highway and on Sep 22 made its radio debut...38 weeks later we all got to celebrate our first #1 song together.

Me and Forest have written a lot together and with some big name writers and have always said we wanted to have our first big hit with a no-name writer...and we got to be that for each other on this song with our friends Kelsea and Josh.

202

Such an amazing feeling to have your first number 1 song...but to have it with your friends that you came up in the business together from the start...makes it that much sweeter! Forest and I both have vision boards that have our name printed off and taped into a Billboard #1 song of the week spot...and now we can print the real thing off and post it next to our dream...proof that dreams come true!" ~LC

MY EYES – BLAKE SHELTON (feat. Gwen Sebastian)

Josh Osborne/Andrew Dorff/Tommy Lee James

1625 Broadway #200

As a lot of songwriters do, Josh had heard another song that he could've sworn was leading up to a completely different hook than it did...in this case, he was waiting for a payoff of "my eyes are the only thing I don't wanna take off of you" in this particular unnamed song, but which never came. So he kept the line for himself and threw it around to some cowriters and eventually found some takers in Tommy Lee James and Andrew Dorff. The challenge

was in keeping the idea "uncreepy" and not having this singer sound too much like a stalker. The solution came when Tommy suggested that they keep it simple, add a sing-along repetition at the beginning of the chorus, and just repeat the hook line. Easy enough approach for another #1 for Blake Shelton.

NEW WAY TO FLY – GARTH BROOKS
Kim Williams/Garth Brooks

1100C 17th Ave S *(see "If The Devil Danced" for photo)*

Kim Williams: "We started this song in a little bit better apartment at 1100C 17th Avenue. We wrote the first verse and chorus and as Garth & Sandy drove back to Oklahoma in his old truck, he said every time he saw birds on a high line he started singing the song all the way back to Oklahoma. When he got back, we finished it and 'New Way To Fly' was an album cut on Garth's second album which has sold close 18 million."

NOTHING ON BUT THE RADIO – GARY ALLEN
Brice Long/Byron Hill/Odie Blackmon

12 Music Circle South

Brice Long: "This song was written in a writer's room at MCA publishing, which at the time was located at 12 Music Circle South. The location is now home to Black River Entertainment. It was written in one of the writer rooms on the 2nd floor in that building. Byron, Odie and I spent about 2 hours writing this song that day before going to lunch. Then it only took almost six years for Gary to cut it and go to #1 for two weeks in December of 2004."

ONCE IN A VERY BLUE MOON – NANCI GRIFFITH
Pat Alger/Eugene Levine

2222 Ashwood Ave

Pat Alger and Eugene Levine wrote this Nanci Griffith title track on the porch of this house. The song has also been recorded by Mary Black, Crystal Gayle, Dolly Parton, as well as The Muppets' very own Ms. Piggy.

ONLY THE WIND – BILLY DEAN
Chuck Jones/Tom Shapiro

Inspired: 1312 Clifton Lane
Written: 10 Music Circle S. #1 upstairs

Chuck Jones: "I got the idea one night while sitting on my couch and reading a book. My wife and I lived at the time in a duplex on Clifton Lane, off of Belmont. It wasn't a bad neighborhood, but was on the edge. We had recently had

break-ins on both sides of us. Probably crack heads from the next neighborhood over stealing stuff to pawn for their next pipeful. But so far, we had been lucky. As I said, not only had the couple in

205

the other half of our duplex been robbed, but the couple in the house next door had been robbed as well.

But there was also the fact that the couple who owned the house next door had recently suffered a terrible tragedy. They were a great young couple, and she worked at a center for mentally handicapped kids just down the street on Belmont. One fine day, she had a day off so she went to Percy Warner park to sit on a blanket and read her Bible. I remember Robin Boswell was her name. A really sweet girl. I didn't hear about the tragic news until I got home from writing at about 9 that night. She had been viciously murdered in the park that day. Bludgeoned in the head with a lead pipe and shot several times. Someone who was collecting leaves in the park found her body. When the police arrived, they saw William Clark Dugger attempting to leave in Robin's car. He was apprehended a short time later. He confessed to her murder as well as to the kidnapping and attempted murder of Andrea Conte, who had escaped from his moving car several months earlier. All though this event had happened in 1989, it was still very heavy on my mind, having happened to someone who lived right next door.

So, I was sitting on the couch reading a book in the living room, with the window opened behind me, as it was a nice cool night. My wife was asleep in the bedroom. It was late. One neighbor had just installed painful B&E prevention devices on his windows and the other, on the opposite side of our duplex, had just been broken into a few nights prior. Suddenly I heard a noise in the bushes outside the open window. I was so on edge I practically jumped out of my skin. So, I very carefully walked outside to investigate. Storms were approaching and much to my relief, the noise I had heard in the bushes was 'only the wind'. That was my exact thought, so I immediately added that phrase to my title page. ;)

I was writing with Tom Shapiro a couple of weeks later and I just handed him that title page and he picked that one. This song was written in the same room upstairs at Sound Stage as mentioned already. Tom had been listening to the new Bruce Springsteen CD. It had a song on it called "One Step Up (And Two Steps Back)". He liked that feel and those changes, so that was our starting point musically. Tom was also co-producing a new Capitol artist, Billy Dean, with Chuck Howard. The song was recorded a few weeks later, right downstairs. I got to play acoustic guitar on the record."

OVERNIGHT MALE – GEORGE STRAIT
Kim Williams/Rich Fagan/Ron Harbin

1100C 17th Ave S. *(see "If The Devil Danced" for photo)*

Kim Williams: "Ron called me at 6 AM and I had just finished 2 miles on my treadmill. Ron had bought an 'Adverteasing' game and asked what I thought of the hook 'Overnight Male'. I said I loved it and we hung up and I got in the shower and started the staccato chorus with the rhythm of the shower. We got with Richard Fagan and finished it. It was in the George Strait movie "Pure Country".

PAPA LOVED MAMA – GARTH BROOKS
Kim Williams/Garth Brooks

1207 17th Ave. S, Apt. C

Kim Williams: "We wrote this song at Benay apartments at 1207 17th Ave. South, Apt. C. The place had a roach problem and we were having a 'modus operandi' problem. We had Papa as an engineer and didn't know how he was gonna kill Mama so Garth & I decided that 'Daddy' was a truck driver and he would drive his 18 wheeler through the motel room where 'Mama' & her lover were shacking up. We laughed so hard that we were on the floor with these dead and half-dead roaches laying there in stitches. When we were writing 'Ain't Going Down' at Kent's home, we had an attack of termites. Garth told Kent (who was upset that his house was infested even though he had a termite letter), 'Kent, Kim & I wrote "Papa Loved Mama" in a roach infested apartment and it ended up # 1.' That seemed to soothe Kent's emotions and the song turned out to be number 1."

PICKIN' UP STRANGERS – JOHNNY LEE
Byron Hill

4225 Harding Pike, 3rd Floor

Byron Hill: "During the summer of 1980, I had been given an assignment by my publisher Gerry Teifer, to write a song for the movie *Coast To Coast*, starring Robert Blake and Dyan Cannon. I took a copy of the script home. I had only 24

hours to read the script, write the song, do a work tape, and get the song on the plane to Los Angeles. I wrote an entire song by midnight that I thought may work, but I had some doubts about it. I went to bed and set my alarm for 4:00am. I decided to trash the first song, then 'Pickin' Up Strangers' fell out of my head in about 15 minutes. I hurriedly left my apartment on

West End for the office. I got there about 6:00am and went into the little studio there to do a work tape. I had the song on the plane that afternoon and the producers in L.A. loved it. It was recorded by Johnny Lee very soon thereafter, and eventually was released on the soundtrack LP, then as a single (twice), and caused the re-mastering of Johnny Lee's *Lookin' For Love* LP, which was pulled briefly from distribution after 100,000 units or so were released. They re-mastered the LP to include my song. I now have two *Lookin' For Love* albums on my shelf, one with 'Pickin' Up Strangers' on the LP, the other without. The song that they deleted from the LP, became the B-Side of 'Pickin' Up Strangers'. I remember back then fearing the day that I would ever meet Donny Lowery, the writer of the deleted song. Many years later, Donny and I laughed about it. Great guy."

PRETTY WOMAN – ROY ORBISON
Roy Orbison/Bill Dees

1916 8th Ave S

According to Rodney Crowell, Roy was simply sitting in the very top floor of this house, looking out the window, when he saw a pretty woman walk by. He started working on the song and wrote most of it in that sitting.

THE RIVER – GARTH BROOKS
Victoria Shaw/Garth Brooks

810 McCarn Dr.

Victoria Shaw: "Garth came over to write...we were blank for hours with nothing coming out. Finally, he said 'What are you listening to?' and I said 'I'm listening to this new James Taylor album I just bought.' So we put on James Taylor, listened to a few songs and it kinda got us in that folky mood. And then he said 'Turn it off, I've got something' and he started playing the first couple lines of 'The River'. Two hours later, 'The River' was born."

NOT IN NASHVILLE:
ROSE IN PARADISE – WAYLON JENNINGS
Jim McBride/Stuart Harris

Joe Quick Road, 1.3 miles east of Hazel Green, AL

Although not a Nashville site, this story is still interesting. The song was inspired by the true tale of Mrs. Elizabeth E. Routt, a local legend of Hazel Green, Alabama. Mrs. Routt lived in a house 300 yards off of Joe Quick Road, with her husband, Alexander Jeffries, both of them surrounded by a profitable 500-acre plantation. Mrs. Routt had been married twice before...but both husbands mysteriously died shortly after the wedding. The same fate befell Mr. Jeffries...as well as her next husband, Mr. Richard Highs, and even the next two husbands, Mr. Absalom Brown and Mr. William Routt.

The rumor remains that Mrs. Routt hung each man's hat in main foyer after their death, so that there was eventually a long row of hats along the hallway.

Elizabeth Routt was tried in Huntsville but was never convicted of the crimes. The house itself burned down in 1968 but a few remnants, such as the fireplace, can still be seen from the main road.

Jim McBride and Stuart Harris were telling ghost stories one day and Jim, having grown up in northern Alabama, remembered this one from his childhood. Waylon made it a classic in 1987, and one that has been covered by Kris Kristofferson, Patty Griffin, Chris Young, and Willie Nelson, to name a few.

SHE WOULDN'T BE GONE – BLAKE SHELTON
Cory Batten/Jennifer Adan

1201 Villa Place – Edgehill Cafe

The first line is written about the red flowers in front of Edgehill Café where Cory and Jen were sitting during their writing session. The entire song was written at the table outside, just east of the front door.

SHE'S EVERY WOMAN – GARTH BROOKS
Victoria Shaw/Garth Brooks

1111 17th Ave S.

Victoria Shaw: "We wrote this in one of the writer's rooms at Major Bob. It came from a conversation we were having and it was just something he said...I don't remember what exactly but I said 'That would be a great song' and we ended up writing that."

SHE SAID YES – RHETT AKINS
Joe Doyle/Rhett Akins
1012 16th Ave South

Joe Doyle: "Rhett had an artist development deal on Warner Bros. Records with A&R staff member, Paige Levy. This was in 1993 or 94. I had recently pitched songs to Paige for consideration to be recorded by members of her stable

of artists. She liked one particular song 'It Ain't Easy Being Me' I had written with my friend Joe Collins. Paige kept the song in her 'good songs' file to play for her artists in the future, who were searching for material. She played it for Rhett, he liked it, which led to our co-writing appointment at 1012 16th Avenue South a short time later. The building was rented to Malloy Boys, a co-venture with BMG owned by Jim and David Malloy who had much success with producing Eddie Rabbit, Kenny Rogers, Dolly Parton among many other hit artists. Upon sitting down for our co-write, Rhett played me what he had started of what would become his Top Ten Single 'She Said Yes'. I liked the verse he had begun and agreed the title of the song could provide us with a suitable destination for a good song.

One of the most memorable moments in writing the song that day, was when I had thought of the line; 'They lit a flame with the match that God had made' to precede the hook; '...when She Said Yes'. I will never forget the look on Rhett's face as he said to me 'you Yankees are good for something.' This, of course, because Rhett was from Southern Georgia and I, originally hailing from Rhode Island. After completing the song, to celebrate, Rhett and I stopped into a Music Row watering hole called Toucan's, which was located at 26 Music Square East, in the same building that would later house Sammy B's and Figlio's On The Row. While there, we struck up a conversation with songwriting legend Harlan Howard, who proceeded to warn Rhett of the pitfalls of making a habit of stopping in for 'cool ones' after co-writes too often. Rather ironic, considering Harlan's frequency of haunting the same type of establishments for similar purposes.

After a short period of time, we demoed the song and pitched it around a little...and it was put on hold by legendary producer Jerry Crutchfield for Tracy Byrd, who was at the height of his career at the time. As young writers, we were obviously excited at the possibility of Tracy recording the song, but as often happens, he eventually passed on the song, but in the mean time, Rhett had left his development deal with Warner Bros. and had secured a deal with the newly re-opened Decca Label, a subsidiary of MCA Records. Mark Wright produced Rhett's album and "She Said Yes" was the 4th single released after two false starts and on the heels of his first radio hit 'That Ain't My Truck'. 'She Said Yes' was released in October of 1995 and eventually peaked in the Top Ten after six months on the charts in April of 1996."

SKIN – RASCAL FLATTS
Doug Johnson/Joe Henry

1514 South Street

Written on back-to-back days along with "Three Wooden Crosses". Giant Records had just closed and Doug Johnson still had a little time left on his contract...so he put his empty office to use at this building and invited some co-writers over.

SMALL TOWN SATURDAY NIGHT – HAL KETCHUM
Pat Alger/Hank Devito

211 38th Ave N

Pat Alger and Hank Devito started this song on the road when Pat was the opening act for the Everly Brothers (and Hank was playing steel guitar for the Everly Brothers). They finished up the lyrics at this house in Sylvan Park - the song reached #2 on the Country Charts and put Hal Ketchum on the map.

214

SOMEDAY – ALAN JACKSON
Jim McBride/Alan Jackson

1010 16th Ave S

Was also the home to Coburn Publishing where Keith Urban signed his first publishing deal.

SOMETHING LIKE THAT – TIM MCGRAW
Rick Ferrell/Keith Follese

1102 18th Ave S

Rick Ferrell: "I had this chorus lyric in my head for about 2 years, that was part fiction, part nonfiction, that I could not find the right melody or groove for. I tried it every which way from a ballad, mid, to a Bo Diddley style uptempo. Nothing seemed to fit or feel like a perfect match and I didn't want to force it since I felt like I had something with the line "BBQ stain on my white t-shirt." It was either dumb and too quirky or could be really visual and catchy with the right melody/beat around it. I had been wanting to get a keyboard for a while, so one day on my way home from a co-writing session I stopped in a pawn shop and found a used Casio for 99 bucks...perfect! Now all I had to do was learn how to play keyboard! Inspired by my new instrument, I immediately took it into my music room, plugged it in, and started stabbing at the keys trying to figure out chords. After a few hours of messing with it I stumbled on to a little melody/groove that I really liked. It was kinda bouncy feeling and sounded a bit Beatles-ish. So I turned on my 4-track cassette recorder and pecked out the melody with 2 fingers.

As fate would have it, I had a writing appointment the next morning with Keith Follese (at Kicking Bird Music, 1102 18th Ave S) – this would be our first time ever writing together with just the two of us in a room. I played Keith the little two-finger melody that I had pecked out the night before, and being a huge Beatles fan, he really liked it! Keith started playing the melody on his piano and it instantly went from sounding like a kindergartener on a $99 Casio to an actual song melody. We agreed that was what we were going to work on and some verse lyrics started falling out very quickly. We didn't know it yet, but these lyrics would end up being the 1st verse to "Something like That." We had been writing the verse lyrics without an actual title or real direction in mind. We were basically writing stream of consciousness and we didn't want to stop the flow. We finished the 1st verse and looked at each other and said, "Where are we going with this now?" That's when I told Keith about the lyrics I had in my head for 2 years about suntan lines and BBQ stains on a t-shirt. So we tried it and it fit like a glove. That's when we started feeling like we might be on to something special! I had a working title called "Something Like That" but I wasn't convinced it was strong enough so I told Keith I didn't have a title for the chorus. Keith opened up his notebook of ideas and out of all the hundreds of hooks and song titles he had written in there over the years he looked up and said, "I got the perfect title for it, Ferrell..."Something Like That!"" I just kinda laughed and thought to myself, "That's crazy, I guess it must be the title for it after all!"

We finished the song and demoed it with a band at Keith's studio and instantly started getting some positive feedback. Over the next couple of months it would get put on and off hold by a few different artist and bands that we will leave nameless. Then one morning we got a call that Tim McGraw liked the song and was actually going to record it for his "A Place In The Sun" album. Needless to say, Keith and I, and everyone at our publishing company, were very excited and keeping our fingers crossed that we'd make the album and maybe even have a shot at being a radio single! "Something Like That" would eventually be the 2nd single released to radio off the album and would hold the No. 1 spot on the Billboard chart for 5 weeks in a row. And at the end of 2009 "Something Like That" would emerge as the most played radio song of the decade in any musical genre.

SOMEWHERE WITH YOU – KENNY CHESNEY

Shane McAnally/JT Harding

1609 17th Ave. S.
Combustion Music – upstairs

Shane McAnally: "'Somewhere with You' was written in the Combustion building in Nashville in the upstairs writing room, which is really like a living room of sorts. It's a pretty good size room, and I had never been in it before, nor have I ever been in it since writing that song. JT Harding had lost his deal at Combustion, and I didn't have anywhere to write, but Chris Farren was kind enough to let us use the room for the day. JT's apartment building was a block behind Combustion, and he was in the process of moving all his stuff, because the building was being torn down. I was borrowing my sister's boyfriend's 1994 Corolla that had a bungee cord holding up the passenger side window. We

were both writing for the pure love of writing. We had no deals, no places to live, no cars...it was really pitiful. We were comparing our recent break-ups, and that song started to flow. JT started singing that shotgun lyric in the chorus, and I couldn't hit record on my phone fast enough."

SUNDAY MORNING COMING DOWN –
JOHNNY CASH
Kris Kristofferson

40 Music Sq W

Previously on this site was the house of Cathy Gregory, an eccentric Nashvillian who rented her upper loft to writers. One of these renters was Kris Kristofferson, who slept in the loft and kept warm by rolling up in the window shade on cold nights. Kris allegedly wrote "Sunday Morning Coming Down" as well as numerous other songs in this loft.

MUSIC ROW: HEART IN THE WALL
40 Music Sq W. Wall around Starstruck

Here lies the "Heart Of Music Row".
Can you find it?

TAKE ME AS I AM – FAITH HILL
Karen Staley/Bob DiPiero

2007 Belmont Blvd – Bongo Java – idea
803 18th Ave S – written

The two writers were having a tough time coming up with a song idea at their session so they took a quick lunch break and headed over to Bongo Java on Belmont. While waiting, Staley used the front restroom and happened to see some graffiti on the wall that said, "Beauty is only a light switch away". She immediately began processing the idea as they finished lunch and headed back to the office (803 18th Ave S). By the time they wrapped up that day, Staley and DiPiero had written the hit that would become the title cut to Faith Hill's breakout album: *Take Me As I Am*.

DID YOU KNOW:
LITTLE BIG TOWN
803 18th Ave. S

A publishing company that was once housed here was called Little Big Town Music Group, where "Take Me As I Am" and numerous other hits were written. A local up-and-coming band sometimes named "Chuckwagon" and sometimes named "Music Buffett" loved the name of the company...so when the company was absorbed and renamed by Sony ATV Publishing, the band took the old name and became Little Big Town.

TEQUILA MAKES HER CLOTHES FALL OFF – JOE NICHOLS
John Wiggins/Gary Hannan

1605 Horton Ave (*see "Anything Goes" for photo*)

It was around Thanksgiving and, as is the annual case, Nashville was winding down for the holidays. John and Gary were taking a break from a slow writing day at Broadway Brewhouse, which would lead to the fortuitous sparkle of insight by the two. John was ordering a round of shots and Gary requested, "Anything but tequila...tequila makes my pants drop". John loved it and pushed to write that title, although Gary appropriately chiseled it to "clothes fall off" instead of "pants drop". The two got together a few weeks later at 1605 Horton and wrote the tune, quickly discovering how tough it is to find a hard rhyme for "off". The song went to #1 in 2005.

220

THAT SUMMER – GARTH BROOKS

Garth Brooks/Pat Alger/Sandy Mahl

Jack's Tracks - 1308 16th Ave S

Another early song written by Brooks and Alger, and also included Garth's wife at the time, Sandy Brooks (Mahl). The majority was written in the upstairs writing rooms of Jack's Tracks.

THAT'S THE WAY I REMEMBER IT – CHRIS GAINES

Tony Arata/Tommy Sims

Jack's Tracks - 1308 16th Ave S

Tony Arata: "I wrote this with Tommy Sims over a couple of sessions. It was started at Jack's Tracks 16th Avenue when I was writing for Forerunner Music. We had already written a song called 'Down In Hollywood' on that day. Before Tommy left, I asked if I could play him a chorus I had – he picked right up on it and the next time we got together over at his office he had fleshed out the verses. We put it down that day as a rough and Tommy's homemade demo of it is what was eventually used on the Chris Gaines project that Garth did."

221

THAT'S WHAT I GET (FOR LOVING YOU)
– DIAMOND RIO
Kent Blazy/Neil Thrasher

1026 Overton Lea *(see "Ain't Goin' Down" for photo)*

Another of the crazy number of smashes written at this house is this Diamond Rio hit. As Kent Blazy tells the story: "I had the idea which sounded like a negative idea yet I wanted to write it as a positive idea. I ran it by Neil Thrasher and he liked the idea of writing it as a positive. We wrote the first verse and wanted to do something different in the chorus so we modulated a whole step in the chorus and then dropped it back down on the 2nd verse. Pretty cool! Neil's a great singer and sings high so his demo sounded like a great Diamond Rio pitch and their producer thought so too."

DID YOU KNOW:
THE ROW
110 Lyle Ave

This space has long been a Music Row hangout, where industry professionals would have a drink and tell war stories from their days in writing rooms and studios. Back in the day, it was a Longhorn Steakhouse (and most recently a Pie In The Sky pizzeria) before becoming The Row. According to The  Row, this is the location where Ronnie Dunn and Kix Brooks first met, paving the way for the most successful duo in Country Music history...and it's also where Earl Bud Lee brokered his deal to pay off a growing bar tab with his publishing of a new song called "Friends In Low Places".

THREE WOODEN CROSSES – RANDY TRAVIS

Doug Johnson/Kim Williams

1514 South Street

Written on back-to-back days along with "Skin". Giant Records had just closed and Doug Johnson still had a little time left on his contract...so he put his empty office to use at this building and invited some co-writers over.

DID YOU KNOW:
THREE NUMBER #1s IN ONE DAY

37 Music Sq. E

Shelby Singleton did the unparalleled feat of recording three #1 records in a single day while based at this location, which at the time was Mercury Records. The three songs were "Walk On By" by Leroy Van Dyke, "Ahab the Arab" by Ray Stevens, and "Wooden Heart" by Joe Dowell, recorded across the street in the Quonset Hut.

THUNDER ROLLS – GARTH BROOKS
Garth Brooks/Pat Alger

Jack's Tracks - 1308 16th Ave S *(see "That Summer" for photo)*

"Thunder Rolls" is another early collaboration between Brooks and Alger also written in the upstairs writing rooms of Jack's Tracks. Recorded in one take during the "No Fences" recording session with Alger playing acoustic guitar.

TIM MCGRAW – TAYLOR SWIFT
Taylor Swift/Liz Rose

123 Cherokee Road, Hendersonville, TN - Hendersonville High School

This is the high school where Taylor Swift was attending math class when she began to hum the melody for her breakout hit, "Tim McGraw". Swift was a freshman here at Hendersonville High School and had been working hard on Music Row after hours, writing for Sony/ATV and recording in hopes of big things to come. She brought her co-writer, Liz Rose, a melody and idea for "Tim McGraw", the first of her trademark "breakup songs", proclaiming the pain of young love and the heartbreak of

innocence lost. This one, incidentally, has to do with a gentleman by the name of Brandon Borello, Swift's senior (at the time) boyfriend who would be heading away to college at the end of the year. The song helped Swift cope with Borello's impending departure and set him up for a lifetime of finger-pointing. Rumor has it, it was completed in approximately 20 minutes on a piano.

UNANSWERED PRAYERS – GARTH BROOKS

Garth Brooks/Pat Alger/Larry Bastian

Jack's Tracks - 1308 16th Ave S *(see "That Summer" for photo)*

A true story that happened to Garth when he went back home to Oklahoma, he and Alger pieced a lot of it together over a few sessions. But it wasn't until Larry Bastian brought in the line "Some of God's greatest gifts are unanswered prayers" did the whole thing come together. Written in Brooks and Alger's favorite writing location: the upstairs writing rooms of Jack's Tracks with Larry providing the key line somewhere on a walk down 18th Ave.

WAKE UP OLDER – JULIE ROBERTS

Lisa Carver

3815 Bedford Ave

Lisa Carver wrote this song on the front porch of the house she was living in at the time, which was demolished and replaced with office buildings.

WALKAWAY JOE – TRISHA YEARWOOD
Vince Melamed/Greg Barnhill

239 17th Ave S.

Vince Melamed: "In the heart of Music row, in the bowels of the old Patrick Joseph Music building, two writers meet for their scheduled session.

Pat Higdon converted a corner of the basement in his old 239 17th Ave S/Division St office into a makeshift writing room/studio for me, and that's where Greg Barnhill and I met in March of 1990 to write. It was fun back then to have most companies run out of old Victorian houses all within a few blocks of each other...this particular building was fairly funky, but we had a great group of writers, and tons of laughs.

Greg came in that day with a title that blew me away, including pretty much first verse and some chorus. I frankly never heard of a "walkaway" anything.

The entire song was finished quickly, (it happens sometimes) with a bridge that didn't need to be there – it never showed up on record, just a nice instrumental break with bridgey chords.

And of course, old genius here made sure that the song demo was mainly guitar, not to scare anyone off those days with piano as the main instrument. Notice that the wonderful Trisha rendition features mainly piano...way to perceive Vinny!"

*Author's Note: This house was another victim of the razing of Music Row...demolished in 2015 to make way for a hotel.

WHAT SHE'S DOING NOW – GARTH BROOKS

Garth Brooks/Pat Alger

Jack's Tracks - 1308 16th Ave S

Written in the upstairs writing room of Jack's Tracks.

WHO ARE YOU WHEN I'M NOT LOOKING – BLAKE SHELTON

John Wiggins/Earl Bud Lee

1605 Horton Ave (*see "Anything Goes" for photo*)

Bud Lee called up John Wiggins with this song idea about who a girl truly is when she's alone, which oddly enough was very similar to one that John himself had written down years before on a cocktail napkin – Bud quickly noted that that was proof that they were meant to write the song together. The pair got together and wrote it at John's Horton Ave condo, feeling that they had something extremely special. The song was originally recorded by Joe Nichols on his *Real Things* album in 2007 but was never released as a single. Blake Shelton, having heard that album and publicly considering the song to be a "career song", recorded it himself in 2010 and took the song to #1.

WHEN I THINK ABOUT ANGELS – JAMIE O'NEAL

Roxie Dean/Sonny Tillis/Jamie O'Neal

EMI – 35 Music Sq E.

Roxie Dean: Jamie and I were both signed to Harold Shedd's publishing company at The Music Mill. We soon became fast friends, co-writer's, then roommates! In that order! Harold had signed Jamie with the intent of obtaining a record deal for her. She was new in town and so was I, and one day Harold suggested we write with his friend Sonny Tillis. So, we did. The three of us instantly hit it off and we ended up writing a lot of songs together...we even got some

228

of them recorded by artists other than Jamie! One day, prior to Jamie getting her record contract, the three of us sat down to write at the old EMI building, which was across from where Sony Records used to be on 16th Avenue. Sonny had a great guitar and melody combination and kept saying "When I think about..., I think about...". It took off from there! We wrote "When I Think About Angels" and knew we had something special. I remember at the time that Faith Hill was looking and we thought it would be perfect for her...well, Sonny and I thought so...but Jamie wanted to keep it for herself. Those are sometimes hard decisions, but we wanted to let her keep it because we knew it could help her career, too (and if you've ever heard Jamie sing, there was no doubt that she would get a record deal). Fortunately, she met Keith Stegall shortly after we demoed the song, and sure enough, it became her second #1 hit and my first #1 hit! We also had the pleasure of being nominated for a Grammy Award. Good times. Thanks, Jamie and Sonny boy!" ~RD

WHO SAYS YOU CAN'T HAVE IT ALL –
ALAN JACKSON
Jim McBride/Alan Jackson

2601 Hillsboro Pk #J14 – The Villager Apartments

When Alan and Jim wrote this song, McBride was going through a nasty divorce, battling his soon-to-be ex-wife, and had moved out of his roomy house, into this so-called "furnished" apartment.
The cigarette-burned furniture, bleak grey walls, and the stark bare light bulb over the kitchen table made an

immediate impact on McBride. Needless to say, "Who Says You Can't Have It All" didn't take long to work itself out.

YOUR LOVE AMAZES ME – JOHN BERRY
Chuck Jones/Amanda Hunt Taylor

10 Music Circle S. *(see "Cadillac Ranch" for photo)*

Chuck Jones: "I wish I could take credit for this title, but it was brought to me by my co-writer, Amanda Hunt (shortly thereafter Amanda Hunt Taylor). It was the first of several songs I wrote with Amanda. It was written in the upstairs room at 10 Music Circle South. The story and inspiration are all Amanda's. As she told me that day, she had just returned from a weekend at the beach with her boyfriend, Rick Taylor. At the end of a great day, while walking on the beach, Rick turned to her, got down on one knee and proposed. While lying in bed later that night, she thought to herself about how his love amazed her, hence the title. Amanda had a musical section to go with the title that she played for me on the piano.

So we wrote the song that first day and my publisher loved it. Amanda's publisher (Kye Fleming) however, thought we needed to rewrite the chorus. I couldn't begin to tell you what the original chorus to that song was. We got together a second time, in that same room, and wrote an all-together different chorus for the song."

230

STUDIOS

After the idea has been born and the words have been written, these are the walls where the music comes to life. There is truly no way to fully encompass all the music that has been recorded in this town. From the earliest days when Nashville's first permanent studio, Castle Records, recorded "Lovesick Blues", to the lobby of the Music Mill where "Achy Breaky" was recorded, and all the way to Blackbird Studios' world-class facilities, there is a rich recording significance around every corner of this town. These are just a very few of the Nashville studios that have made a mark on the world and their magical rooms where the music was made.

ALLENTOWN (formerly JACK'S TRACKS)
1308 16th Ave S

When the nearby Sound Emporium studios got too busy, "Cowboy" Jack Clement bought this property in 1973 for the sole purpose of doing demos and named it "Jack's Tracks". It kept that name for 38 years, even after Allen Reynolds bought it from Clement in 1976. Reynolds used it as home-base for his Forerunner Music venture (with Mark Miller, Jim Rooney, and Terrell Tye) as well as producing acts like Kathy Mattea, Crystal Gayle, and Hal Ketchum. He also recorded tracks by Johnny Cash, Waylon Jennings, and numerous others along the way.

The most mind-boggling tracks that were recorded here include Mattea's "18 Wheels and a Dozen Roses" and Gayle's "Don't It Make My Brown Eyes Blue". Still, it wasn't until Garth Brooks began loyally recording all of his studio albums here in 1987 that "Jack's Tracks" reached cult icon status. Anytime you hear a Garth song, unless it was live, it was recorded in this studio with the band playing live to analog tape a few feet away from Brooks, who was at a simple burlap and foam-covered vocal baffle. Garth even wrote a number of his hits here, such as "Thunder Rolls", "Unanswered Prayers", "What She's Doing Now", "That Summer", and "Like We Never Had A Broken Heart". Tony Arata wrote the Chris Gaines song, "That's The Way I

Remember It" here as well, amongst others.

In 2011, the studio was renamed "Allentown" in honor of Allen Reynolds' industry-changing career. Fun facts include that it had a now-covered swimming pool in its basement that once was office space when room started running out. Clement also filmed the movie *Dear Dead Delilah* at Jack's Tracks, which will give you a peak inside the studio if you can find a copy.

Tours, unfortunately, are not offered.

The legacy of the Civil Wars is thankfully longer than the bright and blinding firework that defined their short tenure. John Paul White and Joy Williams, who met at a songwriter retreat, teamed up with famed producer, Charlie Peacock, at his Art House, Charlie's private studio, to record their Grammy-nominated and winning albums, *Barton Hollow* and *The Civil Wars*. Many other projects, events, and gatherings have been through the Art House to "cultivate creativity" in all art forms – more information can be found on their website, ArtHouseAmerica.com.

BEN'S PLACE (formerly RCA STUDIO A)

30 Music Sq W. Ste 100

www.BensStudio.com

While RCA Studio B gets most of the attention around town, RCA Studio A behind it can certainly hold it's own. The former Javelina Studios is currently leased by Ben Folds, who, for a long time kept it as his own private studio, Grand Victor Sound, unavailable to the public. It has recorded albums and music by the likes of The Monkees, Joe Cocker,  Leon Russell, Waylon Jennings, Dolly Parton, Tony Bennett, George Strait, The Beach Boys, Amanda Palmer, William Shatner (yes, THAT William Shatner), and of course Ben Folds.

The studio came into the spotlight in late 2014 when a developer bought the property, evicted tenants, and were rumored to be tearing the property down in favor of condo developments. Steps for preservation have taken place, thanks to a grassroots "Save Music Row" campaign and a trust being established to repurchase the property.

When visiting the studio, go to the back alley and note the random 3rd floor door floating 20 feet in the air. One of the great urban legends of Nashville was when Bill Hall, the famed of publisher of Jack and Bill Music who was having a hard time getting some material to RCA's Jerry Bradley, used a well-timed and placed cherry picker to knock on this door and hand-deliver the music to Bradley while suspended. Bradley ended up cutting the song.

DID YOU KNOW:
PIANO FROM ORIGINAL RCA STUDIO A

2 Music Sq W
ASCAP lobby

The piano in this lobby is the original piano used in RCA Studio A (now Ben's Place). *Inscription*: "ASCAP acquired this piano from Owen and Jerry Bradley in 1988. The instrument was originally selected by keyboard great Floyd Cramer at the request of RCA Records. Elvis Presley's recordings, most of which were made in RCA, often featured this piano, as did great records made by Chet Atkins, Perry Como, Floyd Cramer, The Everly Brothers, Don  Gibson, Al Hirt, Waylon Jennings, Willie Nelson, Roy Orbison, Dolly Parton, Charley Pride and many, many more."

BLACKBIRD

2806 Azalea Place
www.BlackbirdStudio.com

Perhaps *the* "premiere" studio in Nashville, Blackbird no doubt has one of the most impressive recent client lists. Owned by Beatles fan, John McBride (and his wife, Martina - yep, that Martina McBride), it's hosted and recorded artists/bands such as Pearl Jam, Rush, Kings Of Leon, Jack White, Gaslight Anthem, REM, Taylor Swift, Black Eyed Peas, Red Hot Chili Peppers, Justin Beiber, Kenny Chesney, Bob Seger, My Morning Jacket, Bruce Springsteen, Michael Buble, Lionel Richie, Kelly Clarkson, Bon Jovi, Lynyrd Skynyrd, Keith Urban, Mariah Carey, and an absolutely ridiculous host of others.

The studio is made up of 8 separate tracking and mixing studios spread across a sprawling Berry Hill campus, each catering to a different need and budget. Studio A is the original, more "country" room with a mixing board that came from Hitsville in Motown, as well as a rare adjustable acoustic chamber that has a ceiling ranging from 8 to 20 feet to provide natural reverb. Studio B is where the rock acts typically do their magic. The astounding Studio C mixing room designed by George Massenburg is one of Blackbird's most unique features. With thousands of dowels protruding from the walls, there is not an equal surface in the room, creating a perfectly balanced room and what's described as an "intense" listening experience. Even a priceless collection of over 1,600 vintage tube microphones allows any artist to find the perfect mic for the right voice and project.

Tours are unfortunately not available but, hey, you are welcome to record there if you've got the funds!

BOMB SHELTER STUDIOS

N. 6th St. near Richardson Ave in East Nashville
www.BombShelterStudio.com

The Alabama Shakes made several trips to Nashville to record their critically acclaimed debut album in a house on the west side of N. 6th St. near Richardson Ave in East Nashville, near Cleveland Park. Owner and engineer Andrija Tokic tracked the album throughout bedrooms and back porches while controlling the mix from the dining room. But that was back in the good-ol'-days. The studio has since moved to a larger warehouse setting but the equipment and vibe that gave the Shakes their special sound rolls on in an

all-analog environment that caters specifically to the groove-naturalists out there.

Because the specific address of the original Alabama Shakes recording is the owner's private home, that's as good as we can give it to you for right now. However, if you want the rawest, cleanest analog vibe in town, give Andrija a shout and see if you can capture what the Shakes did.

BRADLEY'S BARN
722 Bender's Ferry Road, Mt Juliet TN

It was on this site that Owen Bradley converted a barn into a studio dubbed "Bradley's Barn" in 1961. Hundreds of legendary artists such as Bill Anderson, Roy Clark, Loretta Lynn, and Conway Twitty recorded hundreds of classics such as "Coal Miner's Daughter", "You Ain't Woman Enough (To Take My Man)", "No One's Gonna Hurt You Anymore", and "Linda On My Mind", among many, many others.

The barn burned down in 1980 but a new studio facility was built on the same spot, clearly visible from the road.

DID YOU KNOW:
CASTLE STUDIOS
206 8th Ave N. (NE corner of 8th Ave N. and Church)

Built in 1894, the Tulane Hotel housed Castle Studios, Nashville's first recording studio with permanent equipment and brainchild of three WSM engineers, Carl Jenkins, George Reynolds, and Aaron Shelton. Although there were numerous locations that recorded music prior to Castle being established at the Tulane, all had portable equipment and were simply make-shift set-ups.

Perhaps most notably, Hank Williams recorded "Honky Tonkin'", "Lovesick Blues" and "Jambalaya" here. The Everly Brothers, Bill Monroe, Red Foley, Ernest Tubb, and a host of others all recorded at Castle.

CASTLE RECORDING STUDIO

1393 Old Hillsboro Rd, Franklin TN

www.CastleRecordingStudios.com

This property once served as a hideout for Al Capone, a rest stop along his travels between Chicago and Atlanta. According to their website, The Castle was "built between 1929 and 1932, the castle sits on 34 cedar-covered acres just 15 minutes south of Nashville and once hosed Capone's bookmaker, John Welch. Since that time, the Castle has served as a bootlegging site, a gambling house, and even an upscale restaurant. But to this day, rumors and legends of escape tunnels and "unofficial" graves still surround the stone edifice.

It was converted to a world class recording studio in 1981 by the Nuyens Family and have served clients such as Alabama, Clint Black, Johnny Cash, Crystal Gayle, Vince Gill, Merle Haggard, Emmylou Harris, Alan Jackson, Barbara Mandrell, Dolly Parton, George Strait, Travis Tritt, Wynonna, Steven

239

Curtis Chapman, Al Green, Third Day, Culture Club, Bob Dylan, Etta James, Jack Johnson, Kansas, Lynyrd Skynyrd, Megadeth, Phish, Snoop Dogg, and Bruce Springsteen.

COLUMBIA STUDIO A
38 Music Cir. S

When Columbia bought the Quonset Hut from Owen Bradley in 1962, it built Columbia Studio A right next door. This studio saw recordings from dozens of classic artists like Johnny Cash, Connie Francis, and Marty Robbins, and was also where Bob Dylan recorded portions of his "Blonde on Blonde" and ground-breaking "Nashville Skyline" albums. The studio was reopened in 2014 as an educational space for students of Belmont University.

Fun facts: A memorable moment that took place in Columbia A was when the band tracked Jeannie C. Riley's classic song, "Harper Valley PTA" with Jerry Kennedy's famous dobro part intertwined throughout. Producer Shelby Singleton apparently made the right call with those dobro licks: the song was released to radio merely 3 days after it was recorded and made Riley the first female to top both the Billboard Top 100 and the Country Singles chart with the same song.

Another note of interest: Roger Miller did a last-minute completion of the song "Husbands and Wives" in the ping-pong room in the basement of Columbia A moments before cutting the song at the Quonset Hut.

CUMBERLAND LODGE

SW Corner of 7th Ave and Charlotte, across from War Memorial

Before there was Music Row, there was the Cumberland Lodge building downtown. Similar to the bustle of the Brill Building in New York City, the Cumberland Lodge housed Mercury Records, Tree Music, the Wilburn Brothers company "Sure Fire", and Sam Phillips' (and later Fred Foster's Monument) studio upstairs. Artists who would just be "hanging out" were the likes of Buddy Holly and the Everly Brothers, not to mention the countless songwriters roaming the halls and inhabiting the writing rooms of the numerous publishers in the building.

A few highly notable recordings here in the upstairs studio are Roy Orbison's timeless classics, "Oh, Pretty Woman" and "It's Over", as well as Charlie Rich's "Mohair Sam".

EASY EYE SOUND
819 8th Ave S

This hidden and very non-descript studio has been owned by Dan Auerbach of the band The Black Keys since their move to Nashville in 2011. While The Black Keys do their share of recording at this private studio, Auerbach opens it up to friends and associates, as well as the acts that he's producing himself, like Brian Olive and The Soledad Brothers.

EDDIE RABBITT STUDIO
1033 16TH Ave S.

Eddie Rabbitt built and operated this studio, which is now Benchmark Studios.

FIRESIDE
813 18th Ave S.

The studio built and formerly owned by Porter Wagoner. Porter produced a number of hits here of his own as well as the likes of Mickey Gilley, Chet Atkins, Marty

Robbins, Shel Silverstein, & Merle Haggard, but its biggest claim to fame is the infamous "Pillow Room". Complete with a mixing board that could be hydraulically raised or lowered, The Pillow Room is where Dolly Parton and Porter would kindly ask the staff to vacate and privately "listen to mixes" in a gaudy room full of pillows, neon, and owls. The room was located up the outside metal staircase. *As this book was going into printing, this studio was torn down to build an apartment complex.

HOUSE OF BLUES STUDIOS (formerly East Iris Studios)

518 East Iris
www.HouseofBluesStudios.com/Nashville

In the heart of the Berry Hill section of town, just a stones throw from Blackbird Studios, sits another world-class studio

complex, the House Of Blues Studios. Not only is it an impressive balance of vintage versus state-of-the-art, but it is arguably the most colorfully decorated and designed studio in town.

Gary Belz bought the famed complex (previously known as East Iris Studios) in 1997 and has been adding to the facility building by building, in some cases having historic structures transported in, which is the case for HOB Studio D. Designed by Norbert Putnam, Studio D was transported by flatbed from Memphis, and has recorded greats such as Stevie Ray Vaughn, Isaac Hayes, and Sam and Dave. The '78 API board is the one out of the Record Plant's black mobile recording truck and was allegedly used to record "Purple Rain".

Studio A is the primary studio, attracting such artists as Barenaked Ladies, Vince Gill, Collective Soul, the Wallflowers, Faith Hill, Janet Jackson, Alan Jackson, Bob Seger, Rush, Matchbox Twenty, and Puff Daddy.

For this author, HOB is unparalleled due to Patty Griffin recording her masterpiece album, *Flaming Red*, here. And for those that need a little more convincing, the party tracks for "Red Solo Cup" were recorded here.

DECIBEL/MIX DREAM STUDIO
118 16th Ave S. Ste 207

When Jerrod Neimann decided to do his own album on his own dime prior to being signed on Arista as a major act, he turned to Dave Brainard, the owner and producer at this non-descript office studio. The vibe

was relaxed, there was no time limit, and there were a few drinks to influence the creativity. For "Lover Lover", Brainard recorded every instrument on the track in his tracking room except for the kick drum, which they recorded in one pass in the adjacent vocal chamber. According to Neimann's biography on GACTV.com, "My original plan was to just sing the lead vocal part. I was going to get Jamey Johnson, Randy Houser, Chris Young and a bunch of my friends to each sing a part. But I didn't have a record deal, and I realized that getting permission for all of them would have been torturous, so my co-producer, Dave Brainard, suggested that I try singing all the parts. I sang eight out of nine parts the first night. The only part I didn't have was that low bass part. I just couldn't hit those notes. So Dave and I went down to the Tin Roof in Nashville, and in the name of country music, we properly medicated the vocal cords.

When I woke up the next morning, I sounded like a mix between Richard Sterban from the Oak Ridge Boys and that cartoon Grape Ape."

Besides Jarrod's first album, the pair completed his second release at the same studio and Brainard has since brought to the studio several highly-touted projects by artists like Ray Scott, and even T-Pain, as well as a Grammy nomination with Brandy Clark.

MUSIC MILL RECORDING STUDIOS |
1710 Roy Acuff Place
www.NashvilleSongwriters.com

A building with a surprising amount of history is the Music Mill, a recognizable log cabin on Music Row that has literally seen true history made within its walls. Harold Shedd build the Music Mill in 1980 after his previous studio on Division (across from the Best Western) got to be too small for his demand. The structure is entirely soundproof, the first to be built on a layered concrete bed that completely absorbs surrounding sound from the neighborhood. The first recording in the studio here was the Alabama classic, "Closer You Get" the first of a record-breaking 21 #1's in a row.

Alabama started the success of Mill, which then churned out Shania Twain (her debut album), Toby Keith (his debut album), K.T. Oslin (her debut album featuring "I'll Always Come Back"), The Kentucky Headhunters, and perhaps the most notoriously recognizable, "Achy Breaky Heart".

"Achy Breaky" was started on Don Von Tress' farm in southern Tennessee but the second verse was written in an upstairs writing room at the Music Mill. The song had already made its rounds in Nashville, having been pitched many times to many artists and even cut by a few before

Billy Ray Cyrus stumbled upon it. When Billy Ray was recording his debut album at the Mill, the producers, Joe Scaife and Jim Cotton, could not find the right sound for the sparseness of the song...one of them suggested that they move the session out to the lobby to get some more resonance so that's what they did. If you walk through the front doors of the

Music Mill and stand in the lobby, you'll be standing in the exact room where "Achy Breaky Heart" was recorded. Just off that lobby is a small storage closet that was the original vocal booth where Toby, Shania, Billy Ray, Alabama, and the rest recorded their vocals for those albums. In the adjacent control room, now an employee office, the vents of the giant cooling system for the monstrous mixing board can still be seen in the floor. The Music Mill has the distinction of having had the first 64-track Focusrite digital mixing board – the best of the best at the time – in the United States. Ron Wood of the Rolling Stones even spent a few weeks at the Mill to learn how to use this new technology and take the knowledge back to his camp.

This is also the building where Shania Twain met John "Mutt" Lange after Shedd suggested Mutt might be able to help Shania find the right sound for her second album. After a number of promising phone calls, Mutt made the trip and the two began to write and record the songs that put Shania on the map...the rest is history.

To further add to its legacy, the Music Mill parking lot is where Harold Shedd first inserted a tape (which he had randomly been given by a flight attendant on a recent trip) into the cassette deck of his car and heard the voice of a young unknown Oklahoma kid named Toby Keith singing a song called "Should've Been A Cowboy". Shedd immediately turned the car around, ran back inside the Mill and made arrangements to meet with Mr. Keith.

The Mill was primarily Harold Shedd's office (and studio, obviously) while he was running Mercury Polygram, Polydor, and finally VFR Records until it was sold in 2005. NSAI managed to scoop it up after a personal plea to Shedd who graciously reduced the price to accommodate their budget and thus allowed the building to further its legacy in the music industry. It is now home to NSAI's worldwide headquarters.

As far as the curious wheel out front, legend has it that if the wheel was turning, a hit was being recorded...and according to Shedd, the wheel was *always* turning.

OCEAN WAY

1200 17th Ave S.
www.OceanWayStudios.com

This unique looking studio housed in the sanctuary of a 100-year old Gothic church has seen artists like Blake Shelton, Brooks And Dunn, Carrie Underwood, Daughtry, Christina Aguilera, the Dixie Chicks, George Jones, George Strait, Lynyrd Skynyrd, Paul Simon, Megadeth, and even the Spice Girls.

Despite the impressive client list, Ocean Way's big claim-to-pop-culture-fame is the legend of Tony Alamo, the eccentric evangelist for the "Church of the Advent" that occupied the space before Ocean Way moved in. Rumor has it that Alamo kept his deceased wife in a freezer in the basement of the

church, attempting to aid her resurrection by shocking her with electricity, and then blaming his congregation for their lack of faith when the experiment failed. Today, the freezer is gone (reverberation plates in its place), as is Tony Alamo - you'll have to visit him in an Illinois penitentiary.

Today, the studio is fully commercial but operates in conjunction with Belmont University's College of Entertainment and Music Business.

OMNI SOUND
1806 Division St.
www.OmniSoundStudios.com

This unassuming studio is in an excellent location but is easy to miss if you're not looking. It's multi-room facility has recorded Taylor Swift, Jewel, Blake Shelton, Kelly Clarkson, Luke Bryan, Trace Adkins, Charlotte Church, Allison Kraus, Steve Martin, Miranda Lambert, Lady Antebellum, Steel Magnolia, Darius Rucker, The Band Perry, and (ahem) Mason Douglas.

QUADROPHONIC STUDIOS
1802 Grand Ave
www.QuadStudiosNashville.com

Norbert Putnam, Elliot Mazer, and David Briggs opened Quadrophonic Studios in 1970 as a "Pop" answer to the new Country boom in Nashville. It initially was a single-room studio that also housed a publishing company, but was later expanded to two tracking rooms and two overdub suites, making it one of the first multi-room tracking studios in town. While other local studios were producing songwriter demos and Country hits, Putnam, Mazer, and Briggs were selling the virtues of Nashville to record labels out of New York and L.A. and bringing their artists to town to record with Gene Eichelberger at Quad. Also of benefit was

249

Norbert and David's idea to have an open bar every night for anyone who wanted to come by. People like Kris

Kristofferson and Jimmy Buffett responded by hanging out, partying at the disco upstairs while recording was happening downstairs.

Part of Neil Young's *Harvest* (including the monster classic, "Heart Of Gold") was recorded here, as was Dobie Grey's "Drift Away", Amy Grant's "Baby Baby", and more recently, a good amount of Taylor Swift's debut album. Taylor wrote a fair number of songs from her first few albums in the Quad Studio C where her producer, Nathan Chapman, had been doing a lot of work at the time. Jimmy Buffett even started recording his first album here, although

production was later completed in Miami to allow for a more relaxed, "beachy" vibe once Norbert realized that Buffett was going to use his own band to record.

Over the years, Quad has been the home of projects by Jackson Five, the Pointer Sisters, Collective Soul, My Chemical Romance, Elvis Presley, Jars Of Clay, Ryan Tedder, Third Eye Blind, Hank Williams Jr., Ricky Martin, Joan Baez, Johnny Cash, Roseanne Cash, Vince Gill, Amy Grant, George Jones, Sugarland, George Strait, Jewel, Garth

Brooks, Kenny Rogers, Toby Keith, T-Bone Burnett, and even Journey. It has remained a constant legacy of Nashville, still rockin' and rollin' after all these years, and just waiting to make more history.

QUONSET HUT
38 Music Circle S (*formerly:* 804 16th Ave S)

If a birthplace of modern Country music can be pinpointed, it would be here, the site of the famed Bradley studio known as the "Quonset Hut", the first studio on Music Row built in 1954. This, of course, was long before it was even considered to be "Music Row" and there were just residential houses up and down 16th Ave. Owen and Harold Bradley had decided that they wanted to explore the industry of film and television scoring so, after they bought the house at 804 16th Ave S. and built a studio in the basement, they then added a metal Quonset hut attached to the back of the house to do the film and television recording. When the basement recording area proved to be too crowded, the Bradley's set up permanent shop in the Quonset Hut and thus began its history.

In it's heyday, the Quonset churned out classic's like Patsy Cline's "Crazy", "I Fall To Pieces" "Walkin' After Midnight", John Anderson's "Swingin'", Lynn Anderson's "Rose Garden", Johnny Cash's "Ring of Fire", "Folsom Prison", "A Boy Named Sue", "Sunday Morning Coming Down", Tammy Wynette's "Stand By Your Man", "D-I-V-O-R-C-E", and George Jones' "White Lightning" (which was actually in the original basement studio), "Good Year For The Roses", "Golden Ring", and "He Stopped Loving Her Today". Hundreds of other artists recorded at the Quonset, such as Loretta Lynn, Barbara Mandrell, Bill Monroe, Ray Price, Marty Robbins, Faron Young, the Beach Boys, the Byrds, Bob Dylan, Buddy Holly, Brenda Lee, Simon and Garfunkel, Ernest Tubb, Conway Twitty, Johnny Paycheck, Roger Miller...the list literally goes on and on.

One of the earliest uses of "fuzztone" distortion occurred on a Marty Robbins Quonset session in 1961 when the mixing board channel that Grady Martin's bass was input into malfunctioned during a take for the song "Don't Worry". The distorted sound, although purely accidental, was loved by Robbins and he insisted they keep it. That same sound was later recreated in the now-popular "fuzztone" guitar pedals.

The Quonset Hut was eventually sold to Columbia in 1962 and remained in use until 1982 when it was converted into office space. Mike Curb came along and saved the day when he bought the space and restored the site, not only to maintain it's historical significance but also to use as a classroom for students of the Curb College of Entertainment and Music Business. Although no trace remains of the original house, a small arc of the current Quonset can be seen from the alley and parking lot in the rear of the building.

RCA STUDIO B

1611 Roy Acuff Place
www.CountryMusicHallOfFame.org

What more can really be said about RCA Studio B? Its reputation most likely precedes itself, as it is easily Nashville's most famous studio (and most advertised), claiming over 35,000 songs recorded there, 1000 Top 10 hits, and 250 Elvis Presley songs.

Initially built in 1957 for the man himself (Elvis) in order for him to have his own Nashville studio, RCA Studio B was Elvis' favorite. He spanned 13 years of his recording life in Studio B and gave us such standards as "It's Now Or Never", "Are You Lonesome Tonight", and "How Great Thou Art" out of this room. It closed in 1977 but was reopened for tours in 2002 after Mike Curb leased it out and donated its use to the Country Music Hall of Fame and Belmont University.

RCA Studio B is the only studio in town that has an official tour that is offered, which can be done through the Hall of Fame. On the tour, you will hear the music recorded here, discover the stories behind some of those recordings, see the wall the Dolly Parton crashed while parking at the studio, witness the unfixed broken cabinet door that Elvis kicked in, and find many of the original instruments used on these classic recordings:

Everly Brothers: "All I Have To Do Is Dream", Don Gibson: "Oh Lonesome Me", John Hartford: "Gentle On My Mind", Waylon Jennings: "Only Daddy That'll Walk The Line", Roy Orbison: "Only The Lonely", "Crying", Dolly Parton: "Jolene", "I Will Always Love You", Charley Pride: "Kiss An Angel Good Mornin'", Jim Reeves: "He'll Have To Go", "Welcome To My World", Connie Smith: "Once A Day", Marty Stuart: "Hummingbyrd", Porter Wagoner: "Green, Green, Grass Of Home", Dottie West: "Here Comes My Baby".

RCA VICTOR

1525 McGavock St

On this site of what's now a parking lot for Beaman Toyota was once RCA's first permanent studio, RCA Victor. Elvis first recorded here under his new contract with RCA on January 10 and 11, 1956, one song being the break-through single, "Heartbreak Hotel". The success of "Heartbreak Hotel" allowed for Nashville to become a credible music hub and

thus began the mass migration of publishing, production, producers, artists, and writers to the town. RCA eventually moved out of RCA Victor in 1957 and into Studio B.

A few other notable events at the studio are Elvis recording "I Want You, I Need You, I Love You", Hank Snow recording a few sessions, and much later on, housing the studio for the *Crook And Chase* show.

Another artist that recorded here was an 11-year old guitar phenom by the name of Jerry Kennedy from Louisiana. Although the album itself never got the attention it deserved, the experience paved the way for Kennedy to forge a relationship with Chet Atkins and to go on to produce Jerry Lee Lewis, the Statler Brothers, Roger Miller, and Tom T. Hall to name a very few. Kennedy was famously the dobro player on the Jeannie C. Riley's classic "Harper Valley PTA" as well as one of the driving guitar licks on Roy Orbison's "Oh, Pretty Woman".

SCENE THREE

2600 Franklin Pike

In the shell of this old movie theater that now sits empty was Scene Three, one of the leading video production facilities in Nashville at the time. Scene Three encountered some tax trouble dating back to 2001 and ultimately liquidated in 2006.

Hundreds and hundreds of Country music videos have been filmed and produced both inside and outside of this location. Garth Brooks' award-winning video for "The Dance" was filmed here and there was even a 2012 sighting of Taylor Swift shooting footage in front of the theater.

SOUND EMPORIUM

3102 Belmont Blvd
www.SoundEmporiumStudios.com

When Jack Clement first set up shop in Nashville – after catapulting the careers of Jerry Lee Lewis, Johnny Cash, and Charlie Rich at Sun Records in Memphis but before he founded Jack's Tracks - he built this studio in 1969, originally named "Jack Clement Recording Studios". The name was eventually changed to "Sound Emporium" and, over the years, it has churned out household recordings like "The Gambler", "Mamma's Don't Let Your Babies Grow Up To Be

Cowboys", "Don't Close Your Eyes", and "When You Say Nothing At All". From 1992 until 2010, the studio was owned by legendary producer, Garth Fundis, where he cut landmark albums by Trisha Yearwood, Robert Plant, Patty Griffin, Yo Yo Ma, and Sugarland. Other notable projects include "It's The End Of The World (As We Know It)" by R.E.M., "Smile" by Uncle Kracker, Sheryl Crow's "The First Cut Is The Deepest", and the "O Brother, Where Art Thou?" soundtrack.

SOUND KITCHEN STUDIOS |

112 Seaboard Lane, Franklin, TN
www.SoundKitchen.com

Not all legendary recordings happen on or near Music Row. Sometimes, they're a bit off the beaten path, which is the case of Sound Kitchen Studios, an unassuming yet gorgeous recording facility just north of downtown Franklin.

Sound Kitchen has been the home to thousands of albums. Some impressive titles include:

Chicago, Keith Urban's *Love, Pain, and the Whole Crazy Thing* and *Golden Road*, Lee Ann Womack's *I Hope You Dance*, Taylor Swift's *Fearless*, Lyle Lovett's *It's Not Big It's Large*, Carrie Underwood's *Some Hearts*, Rascal Flatts' *Still Feels Good* and *Me and My Gang*, Gretchen Wilson's *Here For The Party*, Bruce Springsteen's *The Rising*, Darius Rucker's *Learn To Live*, Dixie Chicks' *Fly*, Gary Allen's *Tough All Over*, Trisha Yearwood's *Inside Out*, Miley Cyrus' *Breakout*, Jewel's *Standing Still*, Billy

Currington's "Pretty Good At Drinking Beer", and even Insane Clown Posse's *Juggalo Homies*. Other bands and artists to record here are Earth, Wind, & Fire, RUSH, Nelly Furtado, Michael McDonald, Jonny Lang, George Strait, George Jones, Don Henley, and Brad Paisley.

SOUND SHOP
1307 Division

In June of 1974, Paul McCartney, his wife, Linda, and their band, Wings, descended upon Nashville to see the town. Curly Putman ("Green, Green Grass Of Home", 'He Stopped Loving Her Today") took a vacation to Hawaii while

McCartney & Co. stayed on his 133-acre farm in Lebanon and toured Nashville, going to the Grand Ole Opry, the Loveless Café, and Printers Alley (dinner at the Captain's Table), all hosted by Buddy Killen himself.

During this time, McCartney wrote "Junior's Farm", a reference to Putman's farm (his nickname was "Junior") and "Sally G" after a night out to Printer's Alley. Although they weren't supposed to be working on their trip, as they had no green card, that didn't stop them from recording a few sessions at the Sound Shop, owned at the time by Killen. They recorded the two freshly written songs as well as "Bridge Over The River Suite", "Hey Diddle", "Wide Prairie", "Send Me The Heart", and "Walking In The Park With Eloise".

The songs appear on the Paul McCartney & Wings bootleg album, *The Nashville Sessions.*

SOUND STAGE
10 Music Circle S.

Sound Stage is yet another historic building that has seen its fair share of hitmakers. Not only is it a fully functioning multi-studio, but it has also been a popular songwriting facility over the years.

Artists such as Faron Young, Patty Pope, George Strait, Alan Jackson, Sheryl Crow, Alice Cooper, and Johnny Rodriguez have all recorded here. Garth Brooks even did a portion of his "Chris Gaines" experiment here.

Jerry Kennedy produced a few of his artists in the Sound Stage studio: the Statler Brothers, Roger Miller, Tom T. Hall, and Jerry Lee Lewis.

Jerry Kennedy:
"The thing about Jerry (Lee Lewis) was that he *wanted* to be produced. He was always one of my idols as a teenager so to be in the same room, producing him, giving him my ideas, was like I was in another world. But we were always right on the same page...something about us really clicked."

SOUTHERN GROUND (formerly Monument Studios and Masterlink)
114 17th Ave S.

It used to be a church...then it was a Confederate hospital during the Civil War...then it was a Confederate morgue...then it was a church again...then it became Monument Studios. And THEN it became Masterlink where Neil Young recorded his albums, *Harvest*, *Prairie Wind*, and *Comes A Time*.

It was also here that the late great Mel McDaniel recorded the hits "Stand Up" and "Baby's Got Her Blue Jeans On".

These days, it's had a facelift, has a new tenant by the name of Zac Brown, and houses his independent venture, Southern Ground.

STUDIO 19
821 19th Ave S.
www.Studio19Nashville.com

According to their website:

"Studio 19, which opened under the name of Music City Recorders in the early 1960's, has seen artists such as Garth

Brooks and Alan Jackson begin their recording careers in our big room. Ringo Starr also recorded his "Beaucoup of Blues" album here. Others like Dolly Parton, Allison Krauss, John Wayne (believe it or not) are among many various artists that have recorded projects here throughout the years.

Scotty Moore, Elvis' guitar player, was one of a group of owners who bought the studio in 1964. Scotty operated the studio until 1975 when it was sold again. The current owners, Larry Rogers and Pat Brewer, bought the studio in 1985. Larry has produced such artists as Ricky Nelson, Brother Jack McDuff, Mel McDaniel, Charly McClain, and Billy Swan."

WOODLAND STUDIOS
1011 Woodland St

For a number of "alternative" artists, they want the Nashville experience and quality...but they don't want to be branded a typical product of Music Row. So they step off the Row, most likely to the ever-growing Blackbird Studios...but back in the day, it was to East Nashville to this reclusive studio getaway: Woodland Studios.

Woodland started off in 1968 with a focus on Country acts:

 Ronnie Milsap, Barbara Mandrell, Johnny Cash, and the Oak Ridge Boys all found Woodland to be their studio of choice simply because it sounded so good.

Charlie Daniels even recorded the monumental classic, "The Devil Went Down To Georgia" in this studio. However, it wasn't long before the Woodland mystique began to attract the less-Country artists like Kansas, Gordon Lightfoot, Neil Young, Bob Seger, Neil Diamond, John Mellencamp, Steve Earle, Elton John, Lynyrd Skynyrd, Dusty Springfield and Ryan Adams.

Woodland luckily didn't forsake its Country roots or the legacy of Nashville itself. The list could go on and on as to who has worked at Woodland through the 80's and 90's: Clint Black, Kenny Chesney, Jimmy Buffett, Radney Foster, Shania Twain, Alabama, Emmylou Harris, Willie Nelson. Today, it is owned by acclaimed artist/writers Gillian Welch and David Rawlings, who purchased the studio after it was condemned in 2001. However, the studio has been completely private since Welch and Rawlings took over. Only a few select artists of a stratospheric caliber – like that of Robert Plant, the iconic front-man of Led Zeppelin – have been able to record a non-Acony Records (Welch and Rawlings' label) sanctioned project...Plant recorded the sessions for his project, *Band of Joy*, at Woodland.

WSM STUDIOS
NW corner of 7th and Union
www.WSMOnline.com

Fitting for the final entry: before Sound Emporium and RCA Studio B...before the Quonset Hut in 1954...even before Castle Studios in 1946, there was this studio: the WSM Studios located on the 5th floor of the National Life and Accident Insurance Company building once located on this corner. No other location or entity in Nashville can be credited with shaping the city into the recording mecca that it has become than WSM, which went on air in October of 1925. Due to its popular show, the WSM Barn Dance, aka the "Grand Ole Opry" (created to advertise and sell insurance, of all things), countless artists and performers would flock to Nashville in hopes of getting their material played on the hit show. As more acts came to town, more recording studios began to emerge, more publishers appeared, more record labels were formed, and Nashville quickly began to grow into a major hub of the music industry.

This building was technically the birthplace of the Grand Ole Opry, since it was simply called a "Barn Dance" in any reference prior to. It was also the site of the first FM radio license in the United States. And it was where an unknown Hank Williams allegedly barged in on Fred Rose's ping-pong game and informed him that he had some songs he thought Fred should hear (although we now know that particular moment in time is popular folklore).

The Grand Ole Opry outgrew the WSM Studios in 1934 and moved locations but the studios remained in use at this site until 1966 when WSM began its own series of studio movements to accommodate their growing industry. The building was torn down shortly after.

One of the biggest disappointments in Nashville preservation is the oversight of this building's mark on history. Although this is truly one of the most historical spots in Nashville, there is only a parking lot on the site. No marker, no inscription, no reference to the fact that it can be pinpointed here that music first began to truly weave it's way into a city that would ultimately become "Music City".

...and now you know Nashville.

BIBLIOGRAPHY

The vast majority of this book was researched through personal interviews. The following resources were also thankfully found and used:

1.) *How Nashville Became Music City*, Michael Kosser, 2006
2.) *Nashville Then And Now*, Karina McDaniel, 2005
3.) "Tennessee Bell Witch", Jan Duke, *About.com*,
4.) "The Hermitage At One Hundred", Ridley Wills II, 2009
5.) "Scuffling: The Lost History Of Rhythm & Blues", Daniel Cooper, *Nashville Scene* Dec 12, 1996
6.) *Lovesick Blues: The Life of Hank Williams*, Paul Hemphill, 2006
7.) "Nashville Songwriter Series: Karyn Rochelle", Rick Moore, *American Songwriter* July 25, 2012
8.) "The People Vs. Jimmy Hoffa", Jim Ridley, *Nashville Scene* March 28, 2002
9.) *Waylon: An Autobiography*, Waylon Jennings & Lenny Kaye, 1996
10.) *A Satisfied Mind: The Country Music Life of Porter Wagoner*, Steve Eng, 1992
11.) *Keeper Of The Clown*, John Cherry, 2013

- www.musicstartshere.org
- www.ScottyMoore.net
- www.hmdb.org
- www.SeeMidTN.com
- www.death2ur.com
- www.findagrave.com
- steveroby.wordpress.com/2012/03/20/becoming-jimi-hendrix-the-missing-footnotes-part-three/
- countrymusichalloffame.org/history/
- www.GACTV.com
- swandive.org/2010/05/wings-over-nashville/
- www.nashvillesongwritersfoundation.com/a-c/sue-brewer.aspx
- tnhomeandfarm.com/castle-gwynn

- http://www.soundonsound.com/sos/apr12/articles/the-civil-wars.htm
- http://www.fiskjubileesingers.org/our_history.html

ACKNOWLEDGEMENTS

This book could never have been written without the absolutely invaluable help from the following. From the bottom of my heart, I give the biggest possible THANK YOU to:

Sherrill Blackman
Jim McBride
Bart Herbison at NSAI
Kent Blazy
Karyn Rochelle
Cory Batten
Charles Green
Harold Shedd
Russ Zavitson
Larry Cordle
Tony Haselden
Butch Carr
Pat Alger
Doak Turner
Judy Harris
Pat Rolfe
Karen Sturgeon
Tony Arata
J. Gary Smith and Devon at Cotton Valley Records
Sam Passamano
Charlie Monk
Chuck Jones
Gary Belz and Tom Freitage at HOB
Ashok Chudasma at the Broken Spoke
Linda Melton at the Elliston Soda Shop

Michael Janas and Chase Geyser at Curb College of Entertainment and Music Business

Nicole Rose at the Drake Motel

Gary Burr

Jerry Bradley

Byron Hill

Vince Melamed

Kimberly Elder at the Hermitage Hotel

Joe Calcaterra III of Cowtown Boots

Jerry Kennedy

Kim Williams

Ken Mellons

Earl Bud Lee

Shane McAnally

Mervin Louque

Judy Rodriguez

Suzanne Lee at ASCAP

John Forcinelli

Nick Shasserre and Scott Phillips at Blackbird

Dave Brainard at Mix Dream Studio

Andrija Tokic at Bomb Shelter

Mark Greenwood at Quad

Karen Staley

Victoria Shaw

Philip Pence

Ronell Venter

Jan Duke

C.J. Hicks

Joe Doyle

Michael Freeman

Shaw Burney

Sharon Haley Bynum

David Butler

John R. Cherry III

Ruthie Cherry

Josh Osborne

Brice Long

John Wiggins

Tom Douglas
Rick Ferrell
Roxie Dean
Matt Alderman
Scott Faircloth
Dennis Barber

Also thank you to the great one, Chris Epting, for telling me he didn't really want to do a book about Nashville, allowing me to buck up and take the reins myself!

And finally to my wife, Kim, for going with me to far more crazy locations than she ever bargained for. We *are* supposed to be here!

INDEX

271

274

S

T

277

Y

Yearwood, Trisha, 45, 53, 54, 133, 146, 147, 184, 197, 226, 257
Young, Chris, 104, 211, 244
Young, Neil, 250, 260, 262

Your Love Amazes Me, 230

Z

Zavitson, Russ, 170, 267

CPSIA information can be obtained
at www.ICGtesting.com
Printed in the USA
BVOW11s0518050817
491160BV00009B/156/P